NO HERO WANTS TO SAVE THE WORLD

How to Raise the Stakes in Your Fiction

ALEX KOURVO

LOVELY DAY BOOKS

No Hero Wants to Save the World: How to Raise the Stakes in Your Fiction

Lovely Day Books

ISBN: 978-1-956107-05-0 (paperback edition)

Contents

ONE

Why Stakes Matter

My favorite movie is *The Princess Bride*, based on the book by William Goldman. It's a story within a story, where a grandfather is reading a fairy tale to his grandson. About three quarters of the way through the story, it seems as if our heroes can't possibly win. Westley is mostly dead. Buttercup is going to have to marry Prince Humperdinck after all. Inigo Montoya won't be able to avenge his father. Things are as bad as they can be.

The little boy listening to the story can't stand it. He wants his grandpa to skip ahead and tell him who kills the bad guy at the end. But the grandpa says that no one kills the bad guy. The bad guy lives.

And the kid loses it. He yells, "Jesus, Grandpa, what did you read me this for?"

I love that line. Every time I watch *The Princess Bride*, I say it along with the actor.

The boy listening to that fairy tale knows what has to happen in order for this story to have a happy ending. He knows what the characters want and he wants it for them. Desperately.

That kid understands story stakes.

Story *events* are things that happen in your novel. Story *stakes* are why they matter.

An intriguing character will bring your readers on board, but it's the stakes of the story that will keep them reading until the very last page.

Interesting Character + High Stakes = Reader Involvement

Once readers are clear on the hero's goal, and what he has to lose, they will read to the end to find out if he achieves his goal or not. If the stakes are unclear, or don't seem important, readers will close the book.

The first thing an author should know when she writes a piece of fiction is what the characters want. This is what readers are reading for. They pick up *Jaws* by Peter Benchley and they want to know if Brody is going to kill the shark that's terrorizing Amity Island. They pick up *The Lord of the Rings* by J.R.R. Tolkien and they want to know if Frodo will make it to Mount Doom to destroy the cursed ring once and for all. They pick up *Emma* by Jane Austen and they want to know if Emma Woodhouse is going to realize that the guy next door—Mr. Knightley—is the perfect man for her.

But just a story about killing a shark? It's exciting, but feels more like a nature documentary than a novel. Hiking up a mountain to destroy some jewelry? Seems like there should be more to the story there. And people fall in love with the boy next door every day.

Luckily for us, literature is complex and multi-faceted. And every successful novel has more than one kind of stakes in it. There are three kinds of stakes in a novel, and your novel needs all three.

There are the external stakes. What the hero or heroine wants.

There are the internal stakes. Why it matters.

There are the personal stakes. Why do we care?

Without external stakes, a story is static. Without internal stakes, a story is hollow. Without personal stakes, a story is flat. Your goal is a narrative where all three kinds of stakes work in concert. When you write, you must know all three kinds of stakes in your novel, you must know how those three kinds of stakes work, and you must deploy the right *kind* of stakes at the right moment.

However, you don't have to know all of this before you start writing.

If you're a plotter (one who works with an outline), you'll usually figure out the three kinds of stakes at the outline stage, and by the time you're ready to write the first draft, you'll know what the stakes are. If you're a pantser (one who discovers the story as she goes), you might start out knowing only two of the three kinds of stakes in your story. You might know only one. That's okay. You'll figure out the other stakes in your story as you write, and when your rough draft is done, you'll have a much clearer picture of the stakes in your novel, and how all three kinds work together.

No Hero Wants to Save the World starts with definitions,

clarifying the differences between the three kinds of stakes so you can pinpoint them in your own novel. Then we'll look at ways to use those stakes in your novel to write a compelling and satisfying story arc. The second half of the book deals with the finer points of narrative, detailing genre considerations, the use of minor characters, and the best ways to resolve the story stakes, making sure your novel ends on a high note.

About the Examples

I learn best from examples, so I've used a lot of them in this book. The most useful examples are the ones that are the most famous, so I've used bestsellers, award-winners, classics, and books that were made into movies in the hopes that these novels are familiar to most people.

My aim is to showcase novels that did something *well*. A good example to follow is always more useful than a horrible warning. Lots of how-to books delight in telling writers what they're doing wrong. I'm more interested in showing writers how to do it right. The only downside is that spoilers abound in these pages. It can't be helped. There isn't a good way to deeply analyze the stakes in a novel without revealing the plot twists. However, I think it's worth it and I hope you do too.

When books are turned into movies, plots and characters often change from one medium to another. Some stories like *How to Train Your Dragon* and *Bird Box* were changed so much when they came to the screen that they're almost a different story. Unless otherwise stated, I'm referring to the novel when I use an example.

My Stakes

I've been a professional editor for over a decade. I've seen hundreds of books in every stage of development. When books come to me for editing, either through the small press I work with or on a freelance basis, the number one problem those books have is that the story stakes are unclear. If readers aren't sure what the hero is trying to accomplish, they won't care if he solves his problem or not.

I wrote *No Hero Wants to Save the World* to help writers like you take a deep dive into story stakes. I want to give you a comprehensive resource you can use to make the stakes in your novels more exciting and more meaningful. I want to encourage you to think bigger, feel harder, and write the page-turning book I know is in you.

My previous book, *The Big-Picture Revision Checklist,* had one chapter on story stakes, giving a brief overview for writers who were in the process of revision. This new book is designed to look at the stakes in your novel at every stage of your writing process, from outline to final draft.

Your Stakes

It takes a lot of work to clearly define your story stakes, and to make sure those stakes are as meaningful as possible by thoroughly exploring your characters' thoughts and emotions. You might be wondering if that work is even worth doing.

Perhaps you feel like you already have a solid handle on your story and you don't want to shake up your plot or take your characters in a new direction. Or maybe you wonder if this will be a lot of work for very little return.

But I promise you that every minute you spend refining the stakes in your story will pay off tenfold. The better you understand the stakes in your story, the easier time you'll have outlining and drafting your novel. Knowing what's at stake makes characterization stronger, plots tighter, and emotions deeper. And a novel with high stakes, developed in a meaningful way, is a novel readers can't put down.

TWO

External Stakes

Usually, when people ask what's at stake in a story, they're talking about the external stakes. This is the big problem that the hero or heroine needs to solve. These are goals like defeating the evil wizard, stopping a murderer, winning a race, winning the beauty pageant, or winning the hand in marriage of the best person you'll ever meet. External stakes are tangible things—you can see, hear, and touch them. And heroes know for sure when they've achieved them. When your protagonist has accomplished this goal, the story ends.

Readers pick up *The Martian* by Andy Weir to find out if Mark Watney will make it back to Earth.

Readers pick up *Bird Box* by Josh Malerman to find out if Malorie and her children will escape the otherworldly creatures and find safety.

Readers pick up *Charlie and the Chocolate Factory* by Roald Dahl to find out if Charlie will finish the factory tour without getting bumped off in some gruesome (but delicious) way.

Sometimes writers make their external stakes too abstract. They think their heroes want "happiness" or "success." But you'll save those for the internal stakes, which we'll discuss later. The external stakes must be concrete. You can test this by making sure your stakes are the answer to a yes or no question. Will Frodo make it to Mount Doom? Will Emma marry Mr. Knightley? Will Brody kill the shark? Things like happiness or forgiveness or self-esteem are not questions your reader can answer. What does happiness mean? Happy for how long? What happens if the hero becomes unhappy? But the external stakes give definite answers to the reader's questions. They know if a shark is dead or alive. They know if wedding vows have been exchanged. And they know if a ring has been destroyed.

However, it's not enough to have something concrete at stake. You have to sell the reader on the stakes you've laid out —why these specific stakes matter to these heroes. What makes the plot of some books sizzle while others only simmer?

Clear to the Reader

Did you ever come into a room where your roommate or your spouse was watching TV and the program was half done? You might watch for a few moments, but you'll have a hard time getting caught up in the story. Even if exciting things are happening on the screen like car chases or explosions, you aren't interested in the outcome. If it's a comedy, the jokes don't land. It's rare that you'll come in halfway through a show and stay for the second half. Why should you? You don't know what's at stake so you don't care.

Readers don't know what's at stake for your heroine *unless you tell them.* I know that seems obvious, but you'd be shocked at the number of times that books have come to me for editing, and I literally do not know what's at stake for the protagonist.

It's going to seem clunky and artificial at first, but readers want this information. You can't be subtle here. You can't expect your readers to read between the lines or intuitively pick up on what your hero wants. You have to tell them. Readers will only care as much as you make them care, and the first step is telling them exactly what they should be caring about, in the most straightforward way possible.

The Silence of the Lambs by Thomas Harris is about FBI trainee Clarise Starling. She's trying to find a kidnapped woman who is in the hands of a serial killer. She needs information from Hannibal Lector, a serial killer himself, who is currently in prison. What does Clarise want? Information. It's right there on the page. Hannibal asks her why she's come to visit him in prison and she tells him why. Now the reader is invested. Is she going to get the information before it's too late?

The White Tiger by Aravind Adiga is about Balram Halwai, who was born extremely poor in rural India. When he gets a job as a chauffeur for a wealthy man, his employer asks him about his social caste. Balram says that there used to be hundreds of castes in India, but now, in practical terms, there are really only two: those with big bellies, and those with little bellies. The rich and the poor. Balram was born with a little belly, and he wants a big belly. Every single thing he does in this novel is about trying to work his way out of poverty and into the upper class. He wants it bad, and that desire is on every page.

If you're worried about being too obvious, you can dress it up the way that Aravind Adiga did. The reader understands what Balram wants, even though he's stated it in a metaphor. Or you can make the stakes exciting by stating the hero's desire in the middle of an argument. Or you can have your hero deny it while his internal monologue is screaming it loud and clear. But somehow, some way, it has to be on the page in black and white in a way that readers can't miss.

Important

The stakes should matter so much to the heroine that it will take all of her time and attention. This should be the most important thing in her life right now. It's what she's spending her time on, it's the number one thing she's working for, and it's basically all she can think about.

This doesn't mean that the stakes have to be important in absolute terms. They don't have to be noble quests like saving the life of a child, or stopping a war, or taking on a corporation that's polluting the local drinking water. The stakes can be "important" only in the heroine's mind. Perhaps she wants to start a skincare business or be chosen class president. The heroine of *Dumplin'* by Julie Murphy wants to win a beauty contest. The hero of *The Sun is Also a Star* by Nicola Yoon wants a girl to fall in love with him. The key is to make this problem loom large in the mind of the protagonist. Your heroine, like all humans, will have many problems, big and small, but make sure that her external goal is *the* most important concern in her life right now. It's so big, it's crowding out all the other problems she has.

In *To All the Boys I've Loved Before* by Jenny Han, the heroine, Lara Jean, has written five love letters to five boys, but has never sent them. The letters were just a way to put her feelings to rest. But her little sister finds the letters and mails them. Now the boy that Lara Jean truly loves knows the truth. The problem? He's her older sister's boyfriend. In order to convince him that it was only a childhood crush and she doesn't have feelings for him any longer, Lara Jean invents a fake relationship with the most popular guy in school. Her one goal is to not come between her sister and her sister's boyfriend. They must never find out her true feelings.

Lara Jean has other problems. Her older sister has gone overseas for college, and Lara Jean is having a terrible time assuming the role of oldest sister. She's afraid to drive, and now she has to. She's having friendship drama with her best friend. But those aren't the problems she's focused on right now. She's got her hands full dealing with the fallout from those love letters and this new fake relationship which is feeling less fake and more real by the day. Next to that, everything else seems small.

In *One for the Money* by Janet Evanovich, Stephanie Plum is trying to make it as a bounty hunter—a job she isn't qualified for. There's a ten-thousand-dollar bounty on an old flame of hers named Joe Morelli and Stephanie is determined to bring Morelli in, but her attempts lead to one mishap after another. Stephanie has other problems. Her wild Grandma is out of control, she doesn't have the equipment or the personal connections she needs to be effective at her job, and she's still attracted to Morelli. When their paths cross, she doesn't know whether to cuff him or kiss him. But those problems seem small compared to Stephanie's need to capture Morelli and claim the bounty. She's failed at so many things in life that she simply can't let herself fail at this, too.

If your hero is fighting or struggling for no other reason than "the story requires it," you're not writing a novel, you're writing a video game. Ask yourself why your hero is doing what he's doing. Why is it important to him? Is he going someplace, or fighting some battle, or having some argument simply because that's the next scene in your outline or because that's what you want to have happen next in the plot? If that's your only reason, take a step back and reevaluate. Because that's how games work, but that's not how novels work. Characters in novels should be doing things for a good reason. They should have powerful needs that are pushing them forward and the agency to go after what they want.

It Requires Sacrifice

If your hero's problem or goal is something he can cross off his to-do list without much effort, then it isn't a goal worth writing about. Novels are about the big stuff, with problems so big that your hero can't help but be changed by them. Readers know this goal is important because the hero is willing to sacrifice just about anything to get it. As you're writing, ask yourself what your hero has given up.

The Underground Railroad by Colson Whitehead is

about an enslaved person named Cora who has escaped from the plantation where she was born. Cora gives up everything in her flight north. She escapes with her friend Caesar, but when they reach South Carolina, Caesar no longer thinks they are in danger, and wants to put down roots. Cora doesn't feel safe, but in order to move on, she has to abandon her friend. Even after reaching Indiana, she can't let her guard down, no matter how tranquil things seem or how strong the black community around her. She doesn't get close to people and she doesn't begin a family. She doesn't even get to keep her name, as she uses a series of false names through the novel. Cora always has to be ready to abandon her entire life at a moment's notice and run again.

But it's not just extreme circumstances that involve sacrifice for your protagonist. It's even more important in light comedies, because you still need to get your readers invested in the heroine's goal. Stakes don't have to be huge but they do have to be meaningful. You can tell the reader that this goal is important by having your heroine give up something else to get it.

In *Legally Blonde* by Amanda Brown, California party girl Elle Woods is dumped by her old-money boyfriend the moment he's accepted into law school. Elle sets out to follow him, and gives up all her fun sorority activities in order to study for the LSAT. Once enrolled, she tries to mimic the preppy students, leaving everything California behind, including her college friends, who were like sisters to her. She soon finds out that she won't get her boyfriend back, and discovers that she doesn't *want* him back. Elle is much more than a pretty face. She's actually quite good at law school, but in order to learn that, she had to change her entire lifestyle.

As you're writing, ask yourself what your heroine has given up in pursuit of her goal. If she can keep her ordinary life intact while still pursuing her goal, then it's probably not big enough or important enough. The story goal should be a new problem in her life that demands new solutions. Your heroine will have to give up something—money, a relationship, a hometown, or a lifestyle—to get what she wants.

A Goal with a Deadline

Without a deadline, there are no stakes. If your hero has all the time in the world to accomplish his goal, then there aren't any consequences for failure. He can simply keep trying again and again. Whatever the hero is going for, he should have one shot at this, and one shot only. Make sure this is your hero's *one* chance to fix this problem or achieve this goal, and that there is a definite deadline attached.

This is easier to see in most genre fiction. In mysteries, the detective needs to find the killer before he kills again. In thrillers, the hero needs to save the city, save the country, or save the world before it's destroyed. In *Lord of the Rings* by J.R.R. Tolkien, Frodo has to throw the cursed ring into Mount Doom before Sauron takes over all of Middle Earth. In *Jaws* by Peter Benchley, Brody must kill the shark before it kills another swimmer.

Some authors struggle to put this same sense of urgency into their literary, historical, or YA fiction. However, there are ways to put deadlines into all fiction, no matter the genre.

In *The White Tiger* by Aravind Adiga, Balram wants to escape poverty. That seems like an abstract goal without a deadline attached. After all, what does it matter if Balram makes money this year or next year, or even the year after that? Eventually he'll make enough to be independent. But the author made that abstract goal very concrete by having marriage hanging over Balram's head. As the matriarch of the family, Balram's grandmother is responsible for choosing his bride, and she's eager to marry him off. Balram knows that if he gets married and has children, he'll be trapped in his tiny village, working in the family tea shop forever. Now it's a race. Will Balram get enough money to live independently before Granny arranges his marriage?

The Sun is Also a Star by Nicola Yoon is about young love. Daniel and Natasha, both high school seniors, should have all the time in the world to get to know each other and fall in love. But Natasha's family has emigrated to America illegally, and they are scheduled to be deported the next day. When Daniel and Natasha meet, Daniel is convinced it's fate and that the two of them were meant to be together. He's sure he can get Natasha to fall in love with him in just one day. As they travel through New York City together, from Harlem to Manhattan, from subways to the roofs of skyscrapers, they go through all the ups and downs of an entire relationship. But can Daniel convince Natasha to risk her heart and be open to love in such a short amount of time?

Be on the lookout for subtle deadlines in the books you read. You'll almost always find a ticking clock of some kind, and the characters will have a finite amount of time to solve the predicaments they've found themselves in. Using this technique in your own fiction will keep readers turning the pages, so find the deadlines in your story and push them to the forefront. You want the reader to feel a sense of urgency as they read, and a ticking clock is the way to do it.

Failure Isn't an Option

Make sure the external stakes have huge consequences for failure. It's not enough to go after a prize or a goal. Your hero needs to fear failure as well. Human beings are funny that way. We'll work to get what we want, but only up to a point. We'll work even harder to avoid loss. This is true for fictional people as well as real ones. As you're writing, make sure to craft your plot in such a way that failure is simply not an option for your hero. If your hero doesn't succeed at this goal, he loses *everything*.

Sometimes writers think "the bad guy will get away with it" is the consequence. But that isn't enough. People get away with horrible things all the time, and at the end of the day, the heroine won't be any worse off simply because someone else did a bad thing. The goal has to affect her personally, and the consequences for failure need to be severe. If the heroine can fail at her goal, and then go right back to her ordinary life no worse for wear, you have some rewriting to do.

The ultimate consequence for failure in every successful novel is death. Every single one. Sometimes it's literal death that's at stake, sometimes it's symbolic, but your novel must have life-or-death consequences of some kind.

In *The Martian* by Andy Weir, astronaut Mark Watney has to escape Mars before he starves to death. In *The Hunger*

Games by Suzanne Collins, Katniss Everdeen either has to win the Hunger Games or die trying. In *How to Train Your Dragon* by Cressida Cowell, Hiccup must capture and train a dragon or face exile—which in his frozen and desolate homeland means almost certain death. These are very concrete life-or-death scenarios.

However, the life-or-death consequences can also be symbolic. You can use death of a career, or freedom, or safety. Death of a relationship or one's social standing. Even death of a sense of self.

The Joy Luck Club by Amy Tan is about four women who have emigrated from China to San Francisco and have formed a social club. They are all raising daughters, and trying to instill traditional Chinese values in them. However, their American daughters think of their mothers as old-fashioned and they don't appreciate the sacrifices their mothers have made for them. Why should they learn to speak Chinese or cook Chinese food or marry Chinese men? They are American through and through.

There are two stories going on here, with two things at stake. The mothers wonder why they worked so hard and gave up so much just so their daughters could run wild in America. The stakes for the mothers are the loss of their culture and their influence. To lose their culture would feel like death to them. For the daughters, the stakes are independence and the constant pull between two worlds. How can they be both good Chinese daughters and modern American women? There is no way to fully live two lives, and failure to resolve that fracture will feel like a death of part of them.

The life-or-death stakes are symbolic in *The Joy Luck*

Club, but Amy Tan has infused her novel with such emotion and depth of character that the reader feels how high the stakes are. These characters have reached their breaking point, and if they don't learn to understand and appreciate one another, the mother-daughter relationships will die.

There is a different kind of mother-daughter relationship in *The Case of the Missing Marquess* by Nancy Springer. Enola Holmes, the much-younger sister of Sherlock Holmes, was raised by her mother and the two are extremely close, so when her mother disappears on her fourteenth birthday, Enola has no choice but to go looking for her. Her father is dead and she hasn't seen her older brothers in ten years, so her mom is the only family she has. Failure to find her mother would be a sort of death to her.

As you're writing, think about a failure that will mean either literal or symbolic death for your heroine. That's what needs to be at stake in your story.

No Backsies

People break their New Year's resolutions all the time. Sometimes the new habits last until February and a few people make it to March, but most people don't last beyond that. People start exercise programs they don't keep up with, say they're going to quit smoking and then don't, or sign up for seminars and self-paced classes that they don't finish.

It's very hard to get someone to change direction in their life. Moving toward a goal is extremely hard and most people won't stick with things long enough to make lasting change. It's much easier to justify the status quo than to shake it up.

One cigarette won't hurt. One more episode of this TV show rather than a trip to the gym. And who cares if I finish that online class or not? There are no real consequences for failure.

Fictional characters need to seem like real people, so they should be just as lazy and scared and risk-averse as any real human. However, authors know where they want their characters to end up, so they push them in that direction, making them try again and again, forgetting that there's an easy out that any reasonable human would take.

Rather than give your protagonist superhuman determination, it's far better to give him a one-way path. Set up your plot in such a way that your hero simply can't quit. Give him practical, personal, or emotional reasons to stick with this plot you've given him.

In *The Wizard of Oz* by L. Frank Baum, Dorothy has to follow the yellow brick road to the Emerald City. She doesn't have any other way to get home. She'll either have to take the journey to the Emerald City or buy a house in Munchkin Land and live there forever. (Maybe she can get a job with the Lollipop Guild or something.)

In *The Da Vinci Code* by Dan Brown, Langdon has no choice but to solve all the riddles hidden in the iconography of the Catholic church. He stands accused of murder and doesn't have any other way to clear his name.

In *How to Train Your Dragon* by Cressida Cowell, Hiccup must capture a dragon and train it, or he faces exile from the kingdom. Hiccup doesn't have any alternative, since his society has no other path for young men to follow.

Your protagonist chooses to take that first step. Dorothy

agrees to follow the yellow brick road. Langdon is just as intrigued by the puzzles as he is afraid of the men who are trying to kill him. Hiccup is right there with the other young men of his island when it's time to begin dragon training. However, once the hero is on that path, he has to follow it to the end. He won't have any choice but to finish what he started.

In chapter five, we're going to talk about when and how to apply the exact pressure you need to keep your protagonist moving forward, but for now, just keep in mind that there are no backsies in fiction.

THREE

Internal Stakes

It's not enough to have something in the outside world that the heroine is working toward. Something inside her needs fixing as well. There is some hole in the heroine's mental or emotional or spiritual life that is going to get fixed by the outside events of the plot.

The *external* stakes are concrete things like defeating the evil witch or winning the race. However, the heroine's *internal* stakes are abstract things like finding her courage, coming to terms with a loss, understanding her place in the world, making peace with her family, finding self-respect, or forgiving someone. The internal stakes are what's missing in your heroine's life, and until she figures out what that is, she won't be whole.

This is the heart of your novel. This is what it's truly about. Plot is what happens in your novel, but the true reason readers are reading your novel is to watch your heroine grow and change. Those external events are a means for this wonderful internal transformation to happen.

. . .

Wants vs. Needs

A good way to think about it is in terms of *wants* and *needs*. The external stakes outside the hero are what he wants. The internal stakes are what he needs. In *A Christmas Carol* by Charles Dickens, Ebenezer Scrooge wants money. That is the only pursuit he's had his entire adult life. And he thinks more money will make him happy. That's what he wants. But what he needs is human connection. He needs relationships. He needs love.

In *The Devil Wears Prada* by Lauren Weisberger, Andi is a recent college graduate and this is her first grown-up job. What she *wants* is to survive a year working for *Runway* magazine. Her *need* is to feel like she's "made it" in New York. She needs to prove that she's a big-city girl now and she really belongs there.

Put a pin in this, because we're going to circle back to it. For now, remember that the hero always wants something and he always needs something, but those two things don't collide until much later in the novel.

Primal Needs

The internal stakes are always primal needs—the things that our caveperson ancestors were concerned with. Food and Shelter. Freedom. Belonging. Safety. Survival. Love. These are things that are universal, in every culture in every time period, because these are human needs. Readers are reading your novel to have an emotional experience and by making the internal stakes so universal, you guarantee that the reader will come along for the emotional ride.

The Princess Bride by William Goldman is all about love. Who is worthy of love? How far would you go for love? Can death stop true love? (No, it cannot. It can only delay it for a while.) Love is a primal human need.

Bird Box by Josh Malerman is about safety. What does it take to be safe? How much can you trust others to keep you safe? How much freedom will you give up to be safe, and is it worth it? It's another human need that resonates with everyone.

Legally Blonde by Amanda Brown is about self-worth. Elle starts the novel thinking of herself as just a pretty face, with her self-esteem tied up in her looks. She ends the novel knowing she's also clever, hardworking, and capable. She's multi-faceted, and has grown way beyond her shallow self-concept. As humans, we all need to think of ourselves as capable people, so Elle's internal struggle is something we all relate to.

Be Subtle

When it comes to the *external* stakes, an author should state them boldly and clearly. However, *internal* stakes are different. If you come right out and state the internal stakes, it will come across as preachy. Now is the time to hide the ball, and make the reader work to understand the hero's internal conflicts.

The hero is always aware of what he wants, but he isn't aware of what he needs. It's bubbling under the surface for the entire book, but it's not something the hero expresses. He's hidden those emotions so deeply he's not even aware of them anymore. All heroes have a blind spot that stems from their internal stakes.

But if the hero isn't aware of his internal stakes on a conscious level, and the author doesn't tell the reader what those stakes are, how will the reader know?

You have to *show* the reader the internal conflict through the hero's behavior. Pretend you were writing a murder mystery with a PI who is incapable of trusting anyone. You wouldn't tell the reader that the PI can't trust his fellow humans. You'd show it by having the PI not believe what his informants are telling him, and constantly double-checking his partner's work, and keeping money in an old coffee can under the sink because he's unsure about banks, and driving his girlfriend away by being jealous. You'd probably include flashbacks to the times his alcoholic father promised him things and never followed through because he was on another bender.

The reader would read all of that and think, "Oh, he doesn't trust people. That's going to be a problem." But the hero has no idea. At least not yet. In the hero's mind, it's not that he doesn't trust people, it's that the world *isn't trustworthy*. Protagonists can always find a way to justify their own internal problems. In fact, if you ask them, they don't have a problem. It's the rest of the world that needs to shape up.

The Martian by Andy Weir is about a man who is stranded alone on Mars for two years, but Mark Watney's problems with loneliness started long before he boarded that spaceship. He's an only child with no spouse or significant other. Basically, science is his girlfriend. When he thinks about who he misses, it's the crew of his Mars mission that he misses more than anyone back on Earth. This is a story about loneliness, about that primal need for human connection, told from the point of view of a man who was lonely long before he ever set foot on that spaceship.

But in Mark Watney's mind, he didn't consider himself lonely before he was stranded. He thought he was doing just fine. He doesn't truly start to recognize this hole in his life until the events of the story leave him without any human connection at all.

The Hitchhiker's Guide to the Galaxy by Douglas Adams is about an everyman named Arthur Dent who escapes Earth moments before it's destroyed by aliens and begins an extraordinary adventure as an interstellar hitchhiker. Arthur doesn't fully understand his world, or why people do what they do, or what the purpose of his life even is. But if you'd ask Arthur at the start of the book, his problem isn't that he doesn't understand the world. His problem is that the world is incomprehensible.

Like most humans, Arthur has a primal need to make sense of his life, and the events of the story lead him on a quest for the ultimate answer to life, the universe, and everything. However, the readers are never told about Arthur's internal stakes—they are only shown. At the opening, Arthur's house is about to be torn down, a fact that he's just learned that morning. He lies down in front of it in a desperate attempt to stop the bulldozers, but gets up and leaves the moment his best friend insists he go to the pub for a pint. Arthur Dent spends the entire first half of the novel being gobsmacked by life, being pulled this way and that. The author plays it for laughs, but the point of the story is a serious one. Humans, as a species, simply don't have a clue. But wouldn't it be nice if we did? And what could we achieve if we actually understood the meaning of life?

The Opposite of External Stakes

In many ways, the internal stakes and the external stakes are opposites. When thinking of the internal stakes, you can look at the important aspects of the external stakes and put the word "not" in front of each one. The internal stakes are not clear to the hero. In fact, he's repressing them. He doesn't think of himself as someone who needs safety or love or self-actualization. He thinks of himself as someone who wants to solve this murder case, outrun this dinosaur, or return home from Oz.

The hero has been living with this internal need for quite some time, and therefore, he doesn't think of it as important, or having a deadline, or consequences for failure. He's built sturdy psychological coping mechanisms around it, and if it weren't for the events of the story, he could go on denying this internal need forever. Novel plots are vehicles for character growth, and it's the external events that bring the internal turmoil to the surface.

In *To All the Boys I've Loved Before* by Jenny Han, Lara Jean has pushed aside her crush on her older sister's boyfriend and is determined to treat him like a brother, no matter her feelings. The love letter she wrote him was her way of purging her feelings on paper. Sealing it up in a box and putting it in her closet makes it clear to the reader that she's sealing those feelings away. She could have gone on like that for the rest of her life. Only after her younger sister finds and mails the letter does Lara Jean confront those forbidden feelings head-on.

The Hunger Games by Suzanne Collins takes place in a world where teenagers are randomly chosen to fight to the death on live TV. Every teenager's name goes into the hat every single year. Katniss tries to keep her head down and simply take care of her family by hunting and foraging. She sees no reason to engage with the larger problems of her society. Early in the novel, she says that she knows the system is faulty, but it's not something they can do anything about. If her sister hadn't been chosen for the Games, Katniss would continue to live her life in poverty-stricken District 12, attending the reaping ceremony every year, watching other teens go off to die in the Hunger Games without doing anything to stop it.

In *Emma* by Jane Austen, Emma Woodhouse says she doesn't want to get married. She's already at the top of the social ladder in her small town, so marriage wouldn't increase her standing. She's the daughter of a hypochondriac single dad, whom she adores, and she envisions a long and happy life taking care of him. However, her behavior shows her internal need, as she tries to arrange matches for all her friends. Clearly, she's fascinated by marriage, as much as she denies it. Her matchmaking schemes spin her ever more tightly into the orbit of Mr. Knightley, who lives next door and is the perfect man for her. The events of the plot force her to come to terms with her true desires.

The external stakes are both new and urgent. The hero has never faced this problem before and needs to deal with it right now. However, the internal stakes are old scars that he's been living with for some time, and he'd prefer to never deal with those problems if he can help it, because dealing with those problems would involve changing himself, and who wants to do that? You're going to carefully write your plot to poke at those old wounds, so the hero will have no choice but to change.

Push and Pull

While it's the external stakes pushing the hero forward, the internal stakes are holding him back. He wants the goal you've set for him as the external stakes. This goal is important, it has a deadline, it's worth sacrificing for, and failure is not an option. But at the same time, those internal stakes are bubbling under the surface and they manifest as fear. The hero's want is constantly pushing him forward while he's afraid to go after what he truly needs, so he stumbles again and again.

This push and pull creates the tension you need through the middle of the story. If you think of a novel as having three acts, this is what act two is all about.

However, this doesn't mean that the hero should be indecisive. Stuck characters will sap all the excitement from your story. Characters who are active, even when in the wrong, are better than characters who are stuck. It's better for your hero to come to wrong conclusions than be indecisive and unable to move.

Let your hero make mistakes. The more the better. That push and pull of the internal and external stakes is the reason your hero keeps stumbling. He wants to achieve his goal without changing anything about himself. Why would he? He's not even aware that he has to change. At first, a hero can only see what he *wants*, so that always seems like the correct solution to the problem. Heroes are always very clear on what they want, so they always try to solve problems in the wrong way at first.

An ideal plot sets these forces working in opposition throughout the book. As things change in the external world, the hero resists that change. He messes up, makes his problems worse, which he tries to fix using his old tried-and-true coping methods, which don't work. Once you get this push and pull effect working, the middle of your book will be taut with tension the whole way through.

In *Bird Box* by Josh Malerman, creatures from another dimension have entered our world. Anyone who sees one will kill everyone around him and then kill himself. People survive by living behind blackened windows and wearing blindfolds when venturing outdoors. The heroine, Malorie, is pregnant and living with housemates, including another pregnant woman. She's existing, but not thriving. The other housemates go out foraging, try to communicate with the outside world, and search for dogs they can train, but Malorie doesn't do any of that. Nor does she read books on baby care or prep cloth diapers. She hasn't made a single plan for the future because in her mind, there is no future.

What Malorie *wants* is safety. What she *needs* is to find courage to face a changed world. But Malorie hasn't yet adapted to this new reality. She doesn't quite accept that things are never going to be like they were in the before-times, and her baby is going to be born whether she's ready to be a mother or not. It's not until a creature gets inside the house and kills her housemates that Malorie finds the strength and bravery to fight it off and save herself and the newborn children. Only then does she adapt to the after-times and become the fearless mom this new world needs.

This push and pull between external and internal forces is also present in literary novels. In *Girl with the Pearl Earring* by Tracy Chevalier, the external stakes are that Griet's middle-class family has fallen on hard times and she has to work as a maid in the house of the painter Vermeer. As a maid, she is constantly at the beck and call of people with competing interests—from the children in the house-hold, the other servants, Vermeer's wife, and Vermeer himself, who wants her to sit for a portrait. She's also constantly fending off sexual harassment from Vermeer's patron—a situation that no one in the household has the power to prevent.

Griet has a keen intellect and an artist's eye of her own, but no way to nurture that talent. She's clearly in love with Vermeer, who teaches her about art and allows her to assist him in mixing paint, but only in secret. The tension in the novel comes from the push and pull from the external and internal stakes. Every time Griet shows independent thought or takes independent action, she's punished for it, whether it's a scolding from the other servants, harsh words from Vermeer's wife, or taunting from the children. She then retreats and has to work up the courage to try another independent action. The reader turns the pages to find out if Griet will ever find a way to live life on her own terms.

Key to Solving the External Plot

In the external world, there is an antagonist who is stopping the hero from getting what he wants. That's a given. But every novel has a second, hidden antagonist: the hero himself. Until he changes—his behavior, his way of thinking, his assumptions—he's not going to be able to solve his external problem. No hero achieves his external goal without changing something inside himself. The internal change comes first, then the external goal is achieved.

In *A Christmas Carol* by Charles Dickens, Scrooge doesn't change his ways after the visit from the ghost of his business partner. He doesn't change after the visits from the ghosts of Christmas past or Christmas present. He doesn't see any reason to do so. It isn't until the visit from the ghost of Christmas future, when he sees his own funeral with nobody mourning his death, that Scrooge realizes his pursuit of money has never made him happy and never *can* make him happy. Only love and human connection can do that. His internal change is what allows the plot complications to be resolved and lead to a happy ending.

In *The Hunger Games* by Suzanne Collins, Katniss Everdeen's 12-year-old sister is chosen for the Hunger Games and Katniss takes her place. What she *wants* is to survive the Hunger Games. What she *needs* is to keep her sister safe. The only way to keep her sister safe is to end the Hunger Games once and for all. Because if she doesn't, her sister might be chosen next year or the year after that. But it isn't until the all-is-lost moment, when she has to choose between killing her best friend and losing the Hunger Games, that Katniss decides to take on the larger fight, to destroy the entire system.

The Rosie Project by Graeme Simsion is about a college professor named Don who has rigid routines for every area of his life and thinks of everything in scientific terms. He presents his first dates with a 40-question compatibility quiz, and then wonders why he never gets a second date. What he *wants* is a wife exactly like himself. What he *needs* is someone like bartender Rosie, who is unconventional, spontaneous, unorganized, and lots of fun. Rosie doesn't fit a single one of Don's criteria for a wife, but she's exactly what he needs to shake him up and show him a new way of living. But it isn't until they break up at the all-is-lost moment that Don realizes what a fool he's been and that the perfect woman was right in front of him the entire time.

The hero always figures out his internal dilemma before he resolves the external plot problems. It doesn't work if you try to put them the other way around.

Tied Closely to Theme

When you're trying to find the theme of your novel, look at the inner stakes. That's where you're going to find it. Or conversely, when you're planning your novel and trying to decide on the inner stakes, look to your theme.

If you try to make your external stakes bear the weight of the theme, you'll end up with a preachy narrative. You'll basically be writing a morality play, and those went out of style in the 16th century. Instead, hide the theme in plain sight by attaching it to the internal stakes. You don't need to hit the readers over the head by telling them the moral of the story. Instead, you can show them by having your hero struggle with the internal stakes. Since the internal stakes are never explicitly stated, they are the ideal place to talk about theme.

For example, in *The Princess Bride* by William Goldman, Westley doesn't just want to rescue Buttercup from her kidnappers, he wants to be worthy of her. The theme is true love and what you'll do to be worthy of someone's love. In *Jaws* by Peter Benchley, Brody doesn't just want to kill the shark, he wants to prove that he belongs on Amity Island. The theme is community and belonging. In *The Martian* by Andy Weir, Mark Watney doesn't just want to escape Mars, he wants to rejoin society, and all of Earth is rooting for him to come home. The theme is the value of human connection.

A novel isn't about what happens. It's about how the plot transforms the character. Your hero is going on a journey that pushes him outside his comfort zone and challenges his beliefs. Readers watch him make fear-based decisions over and over, which ultimately leads to disaster. Only then does your hero change for the better, and when readers see that change, they see the theme fulfilled.

Misery by Stephen King is about an author named Paul Sheldon who is being held prisoner by an obsessive fan. She's furious that he's taking his career in a different direction, and she'll only let him go if he writes the exact book she wants to read—a clone of previous books in his series. Sheldon's external stakes are literally life or death. Annie Wilkes is going to kill him if he doesn't escape.

But the internal stakes are more subtle. Sheldon is struggling with his fame and is unsure of what an author owes his fans. Sheldon considers his previous novels trash and he wants to write art, but he's addicted to painkillers and has to burn the manuscript of his new artsy novel before Annie will give him more. But as he writes yet another pulp novel for his "number one fan," dragging it out in the manner of Scheherazade, Sheldon will have to decide if his artistic integrity is worth his life. The theme is in the internal stakes —does an artist have to sell his soul? Once Sheldon fully commits to writing the novel his captor wants, he realizes that he can marry art and commerce into a successful book that he's also proud of.

The internal stakes are really just a metaphor for the theme. You're carefully crafting a plot to invoke change in the hero, and the theme lives within that change. This allows the theme to emerge organically from the story rather than being imposed upon it by the author in a heavy-handed way.

FOUR

Personal Stakes

Lots of how-to books for writers discuss the internal and external stakes in a novel as if that's all there is. However, there is a third kind of stakes at play: the personal stakes, and they are just as vital as the other two kinds.

Personal stakes are found at the opening of the novel. We begin stories here, with the kind of small, everyday problems that seem like nothing more than an inconvenience. This is the kind of thing that your hero deals with all the time, so it's in his wheelhouse and he feels capable of handling the problem. Because solving this problem seems easy, he charges in blindly, not knowing that there are bigger problems just around the corner.

You see this dynamic in all successful novels. Pull any book off your shelf and look at the kind of conflict that's present in the opening chapters. There *will* be conflict of some kind, but what the hero is dealing with is part of his ordinary world. It's helpful to look at examples from a wide range of genres, so we'll be taking a close look at the personal stakes in three very different books.

Human-Sized Problems

The external stakes are the huge, life-altering, sometimes world-altering stakes. But unlike the external stakes, with their life-or-death consequences, personal stakes are more human-sized. Things like a teenager needing an after-school job so she can afford a prom dress. Things like a family deciding whether it's time to take Grandma's car keys away. Things like a new job opportunity coming up, but it will mean moving across the country. Think about the kinds of everyday problems that your character might have, and find one that will act as a springboard to the big external stakes that will come later.

The Devil Wears Prada by Lauren Weisberger is a comic novel about recent college graduate Andi Sachs. Andi wants a job working for a literary magazine like *The New Yorker*. However, the only job she can find in publishing is working for a fashion magazine as the personal assistant to editor Miranda Priestly.

In the opening of *The Da Vinci Code*, a thriller by Dan Brown, American college professor Robert Langdon has just wrapped up a lecture in Paris when he gets a phone call late at night. It's the police, who are asking him to come to the Louvre to look at some strange symbols that a dead man left behind. Langdon is a professor of symbology, so this is in his area of expertise, and he gladly agrees.

Mexican Gothic by Silvia Moreno-Garcia is a horror

novel that takes place in 1950. Mexico City socialite Noemi Taboada has been living off her family's money and not taking her college studies seriously. However, the family has received a letter from her cousin, who lives with her new husband in a remote mountain village. Noemi's cousin has been ill and claims that her husband has been poisoning her. Noemi agrees to go check on her cousin, thinking it will be a short trip there and back.

A job. A consultation. A sick relative. Personal stakes are always on this smaller level and at first, the problem seems very ordinary.

We've All Been There

The great thing about the personal stakes is how relatable they are. I've never worked for a boss that was so bad that she was literally a legend in her field. However, just like Andi Sachs, I have been turned down for a job I really wanted and had to take what was offered. So many of us can relate to this situation.

I've never been called to a museum to decode strange symbols left by a dead man, but just like Robert Langdon, I have been asked to consult in my area of expertise. People ask me editing and publishing questions all the time. This is not an unusual occurrence in my life, and it probably happens to you too. Nurses get asked medical questions at parties. Fashion bloggers get asked about styling tips. And a computer programmer often becomes the family's in-house IT consultant.

I've never been trapped in a creepy house run by

immortal white supremacists. But just like Noemi Taboada, I have been asked to check up on a relative and then report back to the rest of the family. And haven't we all worried about a cousin at one time or another?

Personal stakes are great because they help with reader identification. Readers will say yes, this is a normal thing that happens, and these are normal emotions to have around it. So later, when those big, life-altering external stakes come into play, the reader will already be on board. When Langdon is going all over Europe on a scavenger hunt for his life, or when Andi is being bullied at work every day, or when Noemi is being threatened by her cousin's husband, the reader will already be identifying with the hero or heroine and sympathizing with them. It makes the bigger stakes a lot easier for your reader to accept.

It Feels Achievable

The personal stakes feel achievable. This is different from the external stakes and the internal stakes. With the external stakes, you've got life-or-death consequences and the antagonist is so powerful, it seems impossible. The heroine is going to be dragged through hell in order to achieve her external objective. And the internal stakes aren't even on the heroine's radar at the opening of a novel.

However, the personal stakes feel like no big deal. Andi thinks she can do this terrible job for a year. Then she can put it on her resume and get a job she'll be proud of. It's only twelve short months. After all, how hard can working for Miranda Priestly be?

Langdon thinks he can pop down to the museum for an hour and explain some symbols to the police. He's good at explaining things. It's what he does for a living. These cops don't seem too bright, but he's sure he can get through to them and then he'll be on his way.

Noemi thinks that she will visit her cousin and get her the medical help she needs. Noemi's family has money and connections, so she assumes she'll either be able to get a doctor for her cousin, or convince her cousin to return to Mexico City, where she can get better help.

Life Will Go Back to Normal

At the beginning of a novel, your hero has one small job to do, one small hurdle to overcome, one small personal problem to take care of, and then—he thinks—life will return to normal. It's very important that your hero has no idea what's in store.

If Andi knew that her new boss would gaslight and dehumanize her every single day while making her work so many hours that she loses her boyfriend and all her friends, she never would have taken that job. But she doesn't know. She thinks that after this year, she's going to have the kind of life any English major from Brown University will have—quiet, literary, and purposely unfashionable.

Robert Langdon assumes the police want him for his academic expertise, and has no idea that someone is trying to frame him for murder. He doesn't know he'll be chasing all over Europe looking for clues that will upend centuries of religious teaching while weird monks and academics are trying to kill him. He thinks he'll be flying home to America tomorrow to teach his next college class.

If Noemi knew that her cousin had married into a family of evil immortals, who had built their home and their fortune on the bodies of murdered laborers, and that they'd lured her to the house to trap her there, she'd burn the whole thing to the ground before ever setting foot inside. But she has no idea. She thinks she's going to help her cousin for one week, two weeks tops, and then return to Mexico City and apply to graduate school.

Because they think they're *only* dealing with their personal problems, the protagonists think they can take care of this one small issue and then everything will go back to the way things were. This personal problem is going to lead to things getting much, much worse, but the characters have no idea what's coming.

Keeping it Personal

As you're writing, it's important that you don't tip your hand too soon. The external stakes are out there waiting, but at the opening of the novel, your hero should remain blissfully unaware. Start with smaller, more personal stakes, saving the bigger ones for later.

You'll be using these personal stakes as a bridge to the larger conflict, so make them relevant. This is where you show the reader the unique characteristics and strengths that your hero has, so later, when those bigger external stakes come into play, the reader knows the hero is up to the job.

As the author, you know the terrible situations that you're

about to put your hero in. You're about to change the hero's life forever. But the hero has no idea what's coming. To him, those smaller, more personal stakes *are* the story, and he wants this as much as he'll want anything later. Desire is the start of every story, so your hero starts the story with a goal, but it's not the same goal he's going to have a few chapters from now, when the true trouble starts.

FIVE

No Hero Wants to Save the World

Most writers understand the ways that stakes work in a story, and the ways that the different kinds of stakes work together. Writers have read about story stakes in how-to books and learned about them in classes and conferences.

But there's a mythology that's been built up about story stakes. Writers are often given two pieces of advice, and both pieces of advice are presented as hard, unbreakable rules. Many writers try to follow these "rules," which they can't, because these two rules contradict one another.

These are myths passed down from writer to writer in critique groups, by beta readers, and in some how-to books. I have sat in the audience at writer's conferences and heard agents and editors say both of these things with a straight face.

The first is that the main conflict has to be present in the opening chapter of a novel.

The second is that authors must constantly raise the stakes.

Neither of these are true.

It's time to do some myth busting.

The Importance of Story Structure

In order to explain why these myths aren't true, we have to first drop back a moment and discuss story structure. Most of us are familiar with the three-act structure, with turning points at breaks between each act. Act two is longer than the other two acts, with a big turning point right at the midpoint. Therefore, many writers think of their novels as having four parts of roughly equal length— act one, the first part of act two, the second part of act two, and act three.

A novel starts with a hook. It's a catchy scene right at the beginning of a novel that introduces the hero and the story world. In *Charlie and the Chocolate Factory* by Roald Dahl, we meet Charlie Bucket and his family, including four grandparents who never get out of bed. Charlie is desperately poor and always hungry. In *The Wizard of Oz* by L. Frank Baum, we meet Dorothy Gale, an adventuresome girl who lives with her aunt and uncle and dog in a small house in Kansas, right in tornado alley.

Plot point one is a big event that happens about 20% of the way into the novel that propels the heroine on the story journey. This is sometimes called the doorway of no return or the break into act two. Charlie finds the golden ticket, winning a tour of Willie Wonka's candy factory, and asks his grandpa to take the tour with him. Dorothy's house gets whisked away in a tornado and she lands in Oz, where the only way home is to follow the yellow brick road to the Emerald City.

The midpoint scene happens at roughly the 50% mark and it's the biggest turning point in the novel. On the factory tour, children begin straying from the strict path set out by Willie Wonka, and they start to disappear one by one. Charlie is terrified that he'll be next. Dorothy makes it to the Emerald City, only to be told that she'll have to steal the broomstick of the Wicked Witch before the wizard will send her home.

At about the 75% mark comes the low point called the all-is-lost moment. It's sometimes called the dark night of the soul or the break into act three. It's that time in a story when everything looks bleak, and it seems as though our heroes can't possibly win. Charlie learns he won't inherit the factory despite being the last child standing. Dorothy is captured by the Wicked Witch. At this moment, things are as bad as they can possibly be.

Finally, there is the climax. This happens differently in different genres. Thrillers usually end with the death or imprisonment of the bad guy. Women's fiction usually ends with forgiveness or new understanding. Romance ends with declarations of love. But whatever happens, the stakes of the novel are resolved. In *Charlie and the Chocolate Factory,* Charlie wins the factory and flies away with Willie Wonka in a great glass elevator. In *The Wizard of Oz,* Dorothy is rescued by her companions and together they defeat the Wicked Witch so Dorothy can finally go home.

This is story structure in a nutshell. I've been very brief here and condensed a lot, but you'll find these big turning points in every novel you read. This is not a formula, and not meant to limit you. Good story structure will help you keep things in proportion, so your beginning doesn't take too long, your middle doesn't drag, and your ending pops. But these guidelines are flexible, and many authors have bent them to good effect.

Sometimes, you find the second half of the structure reversed, or turned upside down. This is useful for stories with a negative ending instead of a positive one. In that case, instead of an all-is-lost moment, you'd see the characters have a false victory, where winning is within their grasp, before it's snatched away. The second novel in a trilogy almost always has this kind of structure, because it propels readers to the third book. Readers need to finish the series to know that their heroes will be okay in the end.

But whether it's a positive story or a negative one, this is the basic structure that you'll find in the majority of novels written in English in the Western world. Knowing this structure helps when you're thinking about the stakes in your novel and where to put each of the three kinds of story stakes.

The First Myth

The first myth we need to dismantle is that the *main* conflict has to be present in the opening chapter. We're talking the big, external stakes, that life-or-death fight that the heroine is going to have. A look at your own bookshelf will show you that this is not the norm for successful novels. *Jurassic Park* by Michael Crichton doesn't start with hungry dinosaurs eating people. *The Da Vinci Code* by Dan Brown doesn't start with Robert Langdon running for his life in the worst scavenger hunt ever. *Charlie and the Chocolate Factory* by Roald Dahl doesn't start with Charlie trying to survive the factory tour from hell.

What *is* in chapter one? The personal stakes.

We all know that the opening pages of our novel are critical. This is the hook, where we grab the readers and get them interested in our story. The first chapter has to wow readers so they'll buy your book. Some writers take that to mean that they have to introduce those big, external stakes right in the opening chapters. But you don't have to do that. In fact, you shouldn't. Of course, the hero has to *want* something. He has to have a goal in mind right from the first page. But it's a small personal goal that leads him to the larger goal with the mile-high stakes. At the outset, the hero only wants to do one simple task and then return to the way things were. He's only focused on the personal stakes right now.

If you try to cram the bigger stakes into the opening chapters, you're setting yourself up for failure in two ways. First, there is nowhere for the conflict to go, so you end up recycling the same problem over and over in slightly different ways. This makes the story feel very episodic, like a sitcom that always returns to baseline. Readers don't mind that when watching TV, but they pick up novels with the expectation that they'll get a story with rising action, where things get more complicated as it goes on. You can't do that if you've already shown all your cards in the opening scenes.

The second problem is even worse. If you put your true stakes in act one, your heroine is going to look like an idiot for getting herself into this. If the true stakes were presented up front, any reasonable person would run screaming in the opposite direction.

In *Mexican Gothic* by Silvia Moreno-Garcia, Noemi thought she'd travel to her cousin's house, figure out what help her cousin needed, and then get her that help. Noemi is a kind-hearted person who loves her cousin, so it seems like the right thing to do. Besides, her father has agreed to pay for grad school when she gets back. She's already dreaming of enrolling.

But what if she knew the true stakes at the outset? What if Noemi knew what evil lurked in her cousin's house? If she'd known that her cousin had married into the vilest family imaginable, who planned to use her as breeding stock to enrich their bloodline? And that once in the house, she'd be cut off from all outside communication, never allowed to leave or to get help?

If she'd known the true stakes in the opening of the novel, Noemi would never have traveled to that remote mountain village. Or if she did, she'd do it with all the power that her family and her money granted her. She'd arrive with her parents, armed guards, and the police. Her family would take the cousin out of the house by force, whisk her back to Mexico City, and then begin a full investigation into that creepy family and just how they made their fortune.

Jurassic Park by Michael Crichton begins with Dr. Alan Grant digging for fossils in Montana. His dig site is running on a shoestring budget, with volunteers and grad students doing most of the work. Then a wealthy man named Hammond comes to Grant with a proposition. He asks Grant to come look at his dinosaur park for the weekend to give his professional seal of approval. In return, Hammond will fully fund the dig in Montana. Of course Grant says yes. One little weekend away, and then his dig is fully funded? Break out the champagne!

But what if the author tried to cram the external stakes into the opening chapters? What if Hammond presented Grant with the *true* stakes at the beginning? What if Hammond had asked, "Do you want to come to a remote island off Costa Rica, where you will see several people get brutally slaughtered by dinosaurs, and it's a good possibility that you'll be eaten by one too? And oh, by the way, a hurricane is on its way, so we'll be cut off from all outside help."

Grant would never take that deal. He'd tell Hammond, "No thanks, I'm going to stay right here, digging for fossils. My dig might be underfunded, but at least *these* dinosaurs aren't trying to kill me!"

Even *The Martian* by Andy Weir, which begins with Mark Watney already stranded on Mars, begins with what I'd consider smaller and more personal stakes, at least compared to what will come later. Being left for dead alone on Mars is a huge deal, but in the opening chapter, Watney is only concerned with his immediate survival needs. He needs to patch his spacesuit, get to shelter, and then see to his injuries. All he wants is to survive the next ten minutes. It's only later that he starts dealing with his longer-term problems —how to grow more food, how to communicate with NASA, and eventually, how to get home.

Thrillers often open with a scene from the killer's point of view, but these act as a prologue, teasing the main stakes, while the next chapter is where the true story starts. In thrillers, the opening chapter often finds the hero safely at home, because what's more relatable than home and family? *Kiss the Girls* by James Patterson begins with two short prologues from the killer's point of view, followed by chapter one, which opens with Detective Alex Cross playing piano and singing with his children. His children know he's been scarred by past cases, and want to cheer him up in the way that kids know how—songs and cuddles and gummi bears. Cross is struggling with work-life balance, and is trying to remain fully present with his kids. All he wants for this moment is to be grateful for what he has, to forget the past and to count his blessings in the here and now. These are the relatable, personal stakes that will lead to the life-or-death stakes that come later, as one of Cross' family members is kidnapped by a serial killer.

Your characters aren't cardboard cutouts for you to drag through your plot. They are as real as you can make them, with all the fears and emotions that any human would have. No real person would purposely let themselves get into situations where they'd become dinosaur bait or victims of white supremacists. Your heroes wouldn't either. But they get into those terrible situations precisely because they don't know what is truly at stake. Not yet.

The Second Myth

Now let's look at the second myth, the idea that you constantly have to raise the stakes. Sometimes people will be more specific, and say the stakes have to be raised *at the midpoint*.

Many writers think they need to take whatever was in the first half of their novel and multiply it exponentially. If you started with car crashes and explosions, now you have to blow up a whole city. If you started with someone's spouse cheating on them, now you need to add a pregnancy from that affair and while you're at it, why not throw in a sexually transmitted disease?

That will make things bigger, but will it matter more? Heroes don't even want this big adventure in the first place, so throwing in random complications won't get them involved. However, if you concentrate instead on making the stakes deeper, more meaningful, and more consequential, then the hero won't be able to help himself. He'll have to stay involved. And so will the reader.

So how do you do that? Not by raising the stakes at midpoint. Instead, you'll be *revealing* the stakes. Or, put another way, it's only at the midpoint that the heroine discovers the true stakes. But by then, it's too late.

The external stakes were there all along. Hammond had already created dangerous carnivorous dinosaurs. The Wizard of Oz was never going to send Dorothy home without that broomstick. And the white supremacists had always planned to trap Noemi in the house. It's just that the characters didn't know it.

But now, at midpoint, they do. It truly isn't until the midpoint scene that the protagonist learns exactly what a huge mess she's just stepped in. Now she understands what she's really up against. Midpoint scenes are always filled with action, emotion, and drama. The action is because huge things are happening. The emotion is because those things matter intensely to the characters. The drama comes from the heroine's realization that she has bigger problems than she ever thought possible. She's waded right into the thick of it, involved everyone she cares about, and pissed off the antagonist along the way. She didn't mean to. She was truly only trying to solve one, little, personal problem. But now she's dealing with so much more.

Genre always intersects with story structure and this is true at the midpoint as well. In action-oriented genres such as space opera, high fantasy, or thriller, the midpoint scene is most likely a huge battle or fight. However, not everyone is writing that kind of novel. In genres that are more emotion-oriented like women's fiction, romance, and YA, the midpoint scene still marks the place where the true stakes are revealed, and after that scene, everything becomes harder for the heroine. She might discover a secret, lose a friend, get betrayed, or miss an opportunity. In YA novels, the midpoint scene is often one of public humiliation.

Even in classic romance novel structure, the midpoint scene is a huge turning point filled with emotion and drama. In a romance, the midpoint is where you'll find the first kiss, the first sex scene, or a similar scene that marks the beginning of true intimacy. And yet, the emotions are the same. "Yikes, I'm falling for this person," and "Oh my goodness, my life is about to change."

And that's why the midpoint is so important. It's always my favorite scene in any novel. It's my favorite to read and it's my favorite to write. Authors who write great midpoint scenes are setting themselves up for success, because this scene acts as a sort of tentpole, holding up the entire narrative. Once you harness the power of this scene, your entire novel will benefit.

Fitting Stakes into the Story

Now we can look at our story structure again and see where the stakes come in. You hook the reader with the personal stakes. They are the most relatable and the most realistic, so readers will easily come on board with your story. You reveal the external stakes at the midpoint. That's the big "Oh no!" moment when the heroine realizes what she's really up against.

Between those two points, you're dropping clues all along the way. The big problem is going to reveal itself halfway through the novel, but you'll be foreshadowing it long before then. In *Jurassic Park*, there are hints early on that some dinosaurs have reached the mainland of Costa Rica. In *Mexican Gothic*, Noemi is having nightmares, her cousin's husband is harassing her, and there is talk of eugenics around the dinner table. When the big reveal comes at midpoint, the reader should accept it. They will be just as dismayed as your hero when the true external stakes are discovered, but you should give them enough hints so that this twist won't feel like it came out of left field.

What about the internal stakes? As we discussed in chapter three, the hero isn't consciously aware of his internal stakes, even as they're causing him trouble. But the readers can see it in the hero's indecision. They can also see it in his bad choices. Time and again, when the external stakes are pushing him forward, the internal stakes are holding him back.

But where the internal stakes truly shine is at the all-is-lost moment. A hero getting what he wants isn't going to get him what he needs. And the all-is-lost moment is where that disconnect finally comes to the surface.

The internal stakes are the emotional center of your novel, and if you don't milk the all-is-lost moment for all it's worth, the story will fall flat. At this low point in the novel, your hero feels as if he's farther from his external goal than ever. But the paradox is that solving the internal conflict is the key that unlocks the solution to his external goal.

Throughout act two, your hero has been having a very hard time. Every time he tries to solve his problem, he's either defeated or he makes the problem worse. The reason things have been going so badly for him is because he's been trying to solve new problems using his old methods, and those old coping skills no longer work. He's trying to get this job done on the outside while simultaneously resisting internal change as hard as he can. Time and again, he's followed the path of least resistance, trying to fix things without doing any of the internal work.

Heroes always need to complete that internal change before true success in the outside world. The opposite doesn't work. Let's say that he somehow manages to succeed at his external goal without first closing the hole in his mental, emotional, or spiritual life. What then? He might succeed, but the victory will be hollow. Even worse, it won't last. So what if Katniss wins the Hunger Games? Her sister will still be in danger next year. Who cares if Scrooge buys his shopkeeper a Christmas turkey? He will still be the same old bad boss on December 26th. If Don Winslow of *The Rosie Project* by Graeme Simsion somehow finds the "perfect" wife that exactly fits his criteria, he won't find lasting happiness. He'll end up emotionally stunted and locked in his rigid ways forever.

Your task is to force your hero to take the harder path of personal change by making it the only path left open to him. Things should get worse and worse until he hits rock bottom. Only then does the internal change happen. He's tried taking the easy way out and has failed every time. Without being brought so low, the hero would never have that crucial insight he needs to achieve success. Without that insight, the hero would be going into the final battle using his old techniques, which means he'd lose.

The all-is-lost moment holds up a mirror of truth. The hero is forced to come face to face with who he's become. Is this who he is? Is this who he wants to be? Or does he want to be better? Everything is stripped bare at the all-is-lost. It's at that moment that the hero becomes his most authentic self, with no mentor to lean on, no allies to turn to, and no secrets to hide behind.

In *One for the Money* by Janet Evanovich, Stephanie makes mistake after mistake through the second act. Her mistakes have not only hurt her, but other people. She gets her mentor shot. She uses a sex worker as an informant, without protecting her in any way, and the woman is beaten and nearly killed because of it. She's tricked Morelli and captured him, claiming the large bounty on him, but then the mobbed-up bad guy breaks into her apartment and she's right back to square one. She's helpless. Afraid. A little bit nauseated. All her allies are gone. She's alone with a desperate criminal holding a gun on her, and his goon is on his way over to torture and kill her. Nothing to do but wait. And reflect. And be scared out of her mind. Stephanie thinks this is truly the end. She's done everything wrong and she won't survive this. Her mother was right all along—this job is too much for someone like her.

What makes her finally tackle the bad guy is the sight of her pet hamster and the thought of him being an "orphan." Throughout the entire novel, Stephanie has been struggling with being taken seriously as a competent person capable of this hard new job, while her family, her mentor, and Morelli all treat her like a child. Her mom cooks for her, her dad drives her places, and everyone talks down to her. Even the small-time criminals she's apprehended in her job don't take her seriously. But she's the "parent" of a pet, and being responsible for him is a symbol of adulthood. That reminder gives her the courage to charge a mobster with a loaded weapon. And even though she gets shot in the butt, she makes her escape and saves her hamster and herself. After that, everything changes. She's no longer Stephanie the bumbler or Stephanie the menace. Now she's Stephanie Plum, badass bounty hunter, who can bring in big bounties and take on mobsters. Most importantly, she can take care of herself.

When crafting your all-is-lost moment, be sure to tailor it to your specific story and to your specific heroine. Whatever's at stake has to matter intensely *to her*. There is something missing in her life, or some flaw she needs to change, or something in her past she needs to overcome. The events of the story should be tailor-made to trigger that change in her by making her realize how toxic her previous coping mechanisms have become. As you're crafting your story, keep genre expectations and tone in mind. In one kind of story, it might take a near-death experience to get your heroine to finally do the right thing. In another kind of story, public humiliation might be the key to trigger lasting change.

The final part of the second act is a time to attack your hero's emotional and spiritual well-being, not his physical body. This section of the story is all about the internal stakes, and if he's fighting monsters or running for his life, he won't have time to reflect. He can do all of that running and fighting throughout act two, but now is the time to stop threatening his body and start threatening his soul. Dig deep and get emotional here. This is the time for your hero to face his fears, be truly vulnerable, and embrace the truth. It's not easy to do that sincere gut check and realize that you've messed everything up, so don't worry that the reader will lose respect for your hero when he's wallowing in misery. Facing your deepest fears is brave. Facing the truth about yourself is even braver. And changing for the better is downright heroic.

The vast majority of novels written for a Western audience will follow this pattern. However, for those of you writing the middle book of a trilogy, a noir or grimdark book, or some kinds of literary fiction, you might want to reverse all of this. Instead of the depths of despair leading to victory, you can have a high moment followed by defeat. Instead of the hero learning and growing, you can have a hero who refuses to change and ends up just as stuck as he was at the beginning of the novel.

Why No Hero Wants to Save the World

Think of those huge, life-altering external stakes as a can of worms that your hero does not want to open. The personal stakes are the can opener. This is the start of things. This is what initially gets the hero into trouble, and those personal stakes are going to escalate into something bigger, scarier, more important, something worse.

Some writers make the mistake of having their heroes jump into the main conflict too early and way too eagerly. But no hero *wants* the external stakes to happen. This is actually the worst-case scenario. Katniss Everdeen did not want her sister to be chosen for the Hunger Games. Scrooge did not want to meet any ghosts. Mark Watney didn't want to get stranded on Mars. Alan Grant did not want to meet carnivorous dinosaurs. And Dorothy never wanted her house to be ripped from its foundations and flung into a mythical kingdom.

Because the big external stakes are so scary, and *not* something a reasonable human would willingly take on, some writers try to solve the problem by making the stakes smaller. No hero wants to save the world, but maybe a hero wants to save a school? Or a house? Or his little sister? That seems reasonable, doesn't it? But this solves the problem in a way that is exactly backwards. Instead of making the external stakes small enough for your hero to willingly jump into, you should thrust the stakes upon him. The external stakes need to feel like life-or-death to the hero, and nobody goes out to seek that. It comes to the hero whether he wants it or not. Once you get those stakes working in the right order, you're free to make the external stakes as big as you want.

Once those big, life-changing, external stakes reveal themselves, heroes and heroines will have no choice but to see it all the way through to the end. What they do next depends a lot on what genre they're in, which is the subject of the next chapter.

SIX

Genre Considerations

Stakes play out differently in different genres. In a thriller, the fate of the country might hang in the balance, while a rom-com is concerned about the fate of a relationship. However, it's a mistake to think of one genre as better than another. Nor is one kind of stakes "bigger" than another. After all, when you're newly in love, your relationship feels as big as the whole world. And when you're fighting with your family, that drama takes up all the space there is. No matter the genre, the story that's happening to your characters is always the most significant event in their lives.

Different genres make different promises about the kinds of emotions that will be found in their pages, and the better you serve those emotions to your readers, the happier they'll be. Readers have very specific wants when it comes to their fiction. A reader hungry for a sense of justice will pick up a murder mystery. A reader craving the excitement of first love will pick up a romance. A reader longing for adventure in far-away places will pick up fantasy or science fiction.

Here are some ways that stakes play out in the most popular genres. This list doesn't take every single subgenre into account and even within a genre, there are many exceptions. This is a very broad, general look at the ways different genres typically handle story stakes—think guidelines, not rules.

Thrillers, Science Fiction, Fantasy, and Dystopian

These genres often share characteristics and emotional appeal, so they're often put together. But there are a lot of exceptions. The genres of science fiction and fantasy in particular are very broad. I've read fantasy novels that could pass as romance and science fiction novels that could pass as literary fiction.

However, in general terms, the external stakes in these genres usually involve overthrowing power, saving the world, upholding a government, saving lives, proving innocence, or matters of duty, honor, or war. The plots are often about some kind of regime change—either preventing it or forcing it to come about. The regime can be as big as a kingdom or as small as a mob family. Usually, the forces of the antagonist are overwhelmingly strong, and the way the world is set up, there is no way for the protagonist to win. Literally no way. In order to prevail, she has to change the world. This is quite clear in *The Hunger Games* by Suzanne Collins. The way the games are set up, Katniss Everdeen is guaranteed to lose. So she changes the game.

In thrillers, science fiction, and fantasy, the internal

stakes are things like the heroine coming to terms with her destiny, finding her place in the world, struggling to hold onto her values, trying not to lose her humanity, or living up to a legacy.

Even though the emotional appeal of these genres lies in the excitement and fast pace of the external story, don't neglect the heroine's internal change. Make sure she isn't just saving the world. She needs to have a personal reason for getting involved in act one—like Katniss, who volunteers for the Games to take her sister's place. At the all-is-lost moment, make sure your heroine digs deep within herself for the resolution. Don't let the story end without some kind of internal change for the protagonist.

Literary Fiction, Women's Fiction

Plot is always a vehicle for character change but nowhere is this clearer than in literary fiction and women's fiction. After the events of a literary novel, the heroine will never be the same again. She's so profoundly different that she feels as if the entire world has changed. Objectively, the external world hasn't changed at all in these genres, but the heroine feels as if it has because she's seeing it with new eyes.

The external stakes usually involve family struggles, wealth and poverty, career struggles, language and cultural barriers, or issues of race and class. The internal stakes are things like feeling out of place in the world, overcoming family myths, overcoming past hurt, and self-identity.

Because literary fiction and women's fiction are such inward-focused genres, the author has to do everything she can to make sure the outer story is always moving forward. Readers expect scenes with lots of introspection and beautiful imagery, but it's important that the reader can sense progress. Otherwise, the plot will feel a bit like a soap opera, with lots of agony and conflict but no resolution.

In *Where'd You Go, Bernadette* by Maria Semple, Bernadette hates living in Seattle where she has no friends and no job. She feels like she's disappearing bit by bit, so she runs away from home, all the way to Antarctica, to find out who she really is. Those are the internal stakes, but an identity crisis isn't enough to hang an entire novel on. Therefore, the author made sure the external plot was exciting too. Bernadette's husband and daughter are desperate to find her, and they follow clues and travel far from home in search of her. These external stakes keep the novel from feeling episodic or static.

Horror

If you ever want to see a character have a truly introspective moment at the all-is-lost point, pick up a horror novel. This genre excels at marrying the internal change and the external victory. The entire genre is based on fear. Characters have to find the origins of their fear, face it, and overcome it. At the end of the day, the big revelation that comes at the all-is-lost moment of *every* genre is about overcoming fear—fear of change, fear of the unknown, fear of becoming a different person. So we can all learn a lot from horror novels.

In horror novels, the external stakes are about fighting the unknown, fighting supernatural power, or fighting extreme human evil such as serial killers or clowns. Internally, the heroine is dealing with self-limiting beliefs, finding her own power, or losing her innocence.

In *Misery* by Stephen King, writer Paul Sheldon is being held prisoner by a deranged fan who gets him addicted to painkillers and then forces him to write the book that she wants to read. The external stakes are clear. Sheldon needs to get away from Annie Wilkes. The internal stakes are Sheldon's relationship to fame, and his fear that he'll be a pulp writer forever and never taken seriously. Annie Wilkes is the very embodiment of that fear, as she *only* wants more of the same kind of novels that Sheldon wrote previously. Annie represents all his fans, and the hell they'll give him if he changes genres. Sheldon shows he's willing to face his fear of professional scorn by burning the novel that Annie Wilkes forced him to write, and he manages to kill Annie in the fire as well.

Historical Fiction

Readers of historical fiction want to feel as though they've traveled to another time and place. They don't just want to visit, they want to *live* in these other worlds. The author is expected to provide accurate historical details, especially about objects that the characters use and touch, such as clothing, household objects, and food. At the same time, readers expect to be swept up in events of historical importance.

The external stakes usually involve wealth and poverty, language and cultural barriers, governments in flux, family legacies, social status, duty and honor, or war. The internal stakes are usually about dealing with society's disapproval, choosing between duty and happiness, or being misunderstood because of gender or class.

The Case of the Missing Marquess by Nancy Springer is about fourteen-year-old Enola Holmes, younger sister of Sherlock, who shares his intelligence and keen observation skills. The author uses very specific details to bring readers into the world of England in 1888. The reader sees the horses and bicycles, the hats and gloves, the fireplaces for warmth and china cups for tea. They hear the train whistles and the clop of horseshoes on cobblestones. They smell the flowers in the countryside and the dirty ditch water in London. They feel the punishing tightness of Enola's corset and the way her hairpins stab her scalp.

However, the author weaves in the details without ever making them the point of the story. Enola's mother is missing, so Sherlock and Enola launch separate investigations. Along the way, Enola gets mixed up with a missing viscount, is kidnapped, robbed, and nearly killed. In the end, she finds her mother using skills that Sherlock doesn't have—her knowledge of feminine dress and the language of flowers.

Readers of historical fiction love historical details, and authors enjoy sharing their research, but be careful not to let the details overshadow the need to tell a good story with meaningful stakes.

Young Adult

Young adult novels are under another huge umbrella. YA novels can be anything from romance to science fiction, but the thing that distinguishes a young adult novel is that the internal stakes are always that of identity—a teenager growing up and deciding who she is going to be and where she fits in the world.

The external stakes are often family struggles, school struggles, issues of wealth and poverty, living arrangements, or questioning sexual orientation. But no matter the external stakes, a YA novel always has that search for self-identity at its core.

Dumplin' by Julie Murphy is about plus-sized teenager Willowdean, whose mother was crowned Miss Bluebonnet two decades ago and now runs the beauty pageant she once won. Willowdean, who is constantly judged for her looks, doesn't understand why anyone would willingly sign up for that. So she enters the Miss Bluebonnet pageant with the intent to undermine the entire thing. If she can make fun of artificial beauty standards *and* piss off her mom along the way? She's all for it. Willowdean has some growing up to do, and ironically enough, a beauty pageant might help her do it.

Mystery

In mystery stories, the external stakes are always the same. The hero's external goal is always to find the killer, save lives, and restore justice. Therefore, the personal and internal stakes are crucial. An amateur detective needs a powerful personal reason to get involved and internal stakes that mean she's going to be changed by the story outcome. Even if finding the killer is the heroine's job, such as in a police procedural, there still needs to be something about this case that tugs at her heart in a personal way. Internal stakes in this genre often include the testing of friendships and loyalty, loss of innocence, and whether to keep or reveal secrets.

The Sins of the Fathers by Lawrence Block is the first in the long-running Matthew Scudder series. Scudder is an alcoholic ex-cop who is working as an unlicensed PI. He's approached by a man whose college-age daughter was killed, and even though the killer is dead, the father wants more answers than the police can provide. Scudder takes the job because he has unanswered questions about his own life. Years ago, when he was a police officer, he shot at a robber, but his stray bullet killed a seven-year-old girl. Scudder has never gotten over it and doesn't know how to forgive himself. So when the father of a young daughter comes to him for help, he can't say no. He can't erase the mistake in his past, but perhaps helping to find justice for this other young woman will ease his guilt.

That is the kind of personal connection you need when you're writing a murder mystery. There needs to be some reason for the protagonist to get involved and it's almost always related to the hero's past. An emotional reason for the hero to take on a murder case will have more pull with readers than a logical one.

Romance

The internal stakes in romance novels are always true love and lasting happiness. The story is always about the main characters changing for the better. Meeting their other half and falling in love is what allows that change to happen.

Because the internal stakes remain the same from book to book in this genre, authors need to work hard to make the other two kinds of stakes credible and unique. It's not enough for the hero and heroine to be attracted to one another. You need personal stakes to bring them together while the external plot works to pry them apart.

In *The Rosie Project* by Graeme Simsion, Don Winslow is a lonely genetics professor who has such a rigid way of thinking that he can't see the good that's right in front of him. Bartender Rosie needs his help to find her biological father, and could also use some help organizing her scattered life. Neither one of them plans to fall in love—especially with their complete opposite. But working together searching for Rosie's father means they spend a lot of time together, and each of them brings out the best in the other.

In romance, external stakes are often things like career struggles, family struggles, living arrangements, or the choice between family and career. On the way to true love, the two halves of the couple might struggle with self-worth, overcoming past hurts, or fear of being open and vulnerable. But those internal stakes—true love—are always the reason a reader picked up your book, and you must deliver the happy ending she's expecting.

Mixed Genres

Many authors have trouble classifying their novels. They write things with elements from many different genres, and when the book is done, they don't know what to call it. Is it fantasy-romance-western? Is it YA-mystery-magical adventure?

Here's the secret: every novel is a mix of genres. There is no pure romance, or pure literary fiction, or pure horror. Every novel borrows bits from other genres. I can't remember the last time I read a mystery novel that didn't have a romantic subplot. And lots of science fiction novels deal with the same weighty themes that literary fiction does.

Some mysteries can also be historical novels, such as the Easy Rawlins mysteries by Walter Mosley, and historical romance is a wonderfully rich category of books. However, these are mysteries and romances *first*, with all the tropes and conventions the genres expect. This is different from *Girl with a Pearl Earring* by Tracy Chevalier, which is primarily a historical novel. Mosley's novels appeal to an audience who is looking for mysteries. That audience wants to see stakes of justice, and a community dealing with a murderer in their midst. Historical romance readers want to read novels where the stakes are true love and happiness.

When you're classifying your own novel, think about what's at stake. The fate of the free world? I'm guessing you're writing a thriller, no matter how much romance or magic is in it. Are the stakes true love, and two people changing for the better to be worthy of another? You're writing romance, whether it takes place in the Regency era or hundreds of years in the future.

The Hunger Games by Suzanne Collins can be classified as a dystopian, science fiction, or young adult novel. It has elements of all three, but when it comes down to the stakes, the dystopian wins out. Teenagers are being conscripted into killing each other on live TV in order to secure food for their communities. Those stakes are so huge (and so bleak) they overshadow the other things in the novel. The other elements are still there—the futuristic weapons of SF, the self-identity question of YA—but the dystopian narrative carries the main stakes, and it's what keeps readers turning the pages.

Mexican Gothic by Silvia Moreno-Garcia straddles the line between horror and literary fiction. The weighty issues of racial justice, women's equality, and workers' rights are crucial parts of the narrative. But readers aren't reading the novel as an intellectual exercise. Readers are feeling Noemi's feelings as she's having nightmares, watching the wallpaper move, and finding herself suddenly in another part of the house in the middle of the night even though she's not a sleepwalker. The slow revelation of the family's intentions is absolutely horrific. The issues underpinning the narrative add richness to the tale, but readers have picked up the book to have a creepy experience with scary stakes, and *Mexican Gothic* delivers.

It's perfectly fine to have elements of other genres in your novel. Readers have come to expect that and they love it when authors mix the tropes of other genres in fresh ways. However, there should be one dominant genre that you're appealing to. If you're having trouble finding your story's genre, look to the story stakes. What your hero *wants* will tell you what shelf of the bookstore your book belongs on.

SEVEN

Stakes That Matter, Stakes That Don't

Readers love it when the stakes are built into the premise. The premise of *The Martian* by Andy Weir is "an astronaut stranded on Mars." The strong stakes are already present right from the start. Mark Watney has to survive alone on Mars and has to make a plan to get back to Earth before he starves to death. Add in the internal stakes of his loneliness and need for human connection and you have the makings of a page-turning adventure.

The premise of *The Sun is Also a Star* by Nicola Yoon is "a boy and a girl have one day to fall in love before they are separated forever." All the stakes that the story needs are right there. These high-concept books are easy to understand at a glance. Readers know right away if this is the kind of book they want to read.

However, sometimes the premise of the novel is not enough. Some goals seem like they'd make excellent stakes for a story but on closer examination, we see that they're missing a key ingredient. The goals might be important and the hero might be working hard to get them, but there is no deadline, no consequences for failure, and if the hero fails, he can simply try again. If your stakes are too low, the story will lack tension and the reader won't stick with the book.

The goals listed below are examples of stakes that don't quite work. You *can* use them as stakes in your story, as long as you tie them to a larger, better goal—one with something truly at stake.

Money

Money, by itself, is not a worthy goal. Everyone knows happy poor people and miserable rich ones, so readers won't believe that simply having money is going to make your hero happy. Although money by itself can't buy happiness, it can buy other things and it's those other things that are your hero's true goal. Money is only a means to an end.

In *The White Tiger* by Aravind Adiga, Balram is doing everything he can to rise up out of poverty, but the money is only symbolic. What Balram truly needs is independence. He's temporarily escaped his grandmother and her marriage plans, but now he's a live-in servant and is completely dependent on his employers for food, shelter, and healthcare. They decide his schedule and keep tabs on his whereabouts at all times. Balram tells his employers they are "like mother and father" to him, which is accurate because they treat him like a child. When they try to frame him for a hit-and-run accident caused by his boss, Balram realizes how powerless he is in this situation and vows to get out. He needs money so he can be free.

Your hero, like all heroes, will be constantly striving for a better life, and it's perfectly okay to have money be one of his goals, as long as the hero understands that he truly wants something else, and the reader understands that too.

Heist

Sometimes heroes want to steal things. This can be a heist or caper, where the hero is taking things for his own gain. It can be a treasure hunt, where he is seeking something hidden. Or he can be trying to regain something that was first stolen from him.

These stories often try to be exciting by taking the hero to exotic places with danger around every corner. But a heist, on its own, won't make readers care because there aren't any consequences for failure. The hero can quit at any time, and in fact, would be safer if he did. And what happens if the hero fails? He won't get his treasure. But if he fails, he's no worse off than when the story began, so why does it matter?

Much like the money stakes, this *can* work, but only if you tie the reasons for the heist to something deeper. There must be personal reasons for the hero to go on this quest and dire consequences if he fails.

In *The Da Vinci Code* by Dan Brown, Langdon isn't just hunting for the holy grail. He's trying to prove he didn't murder Louvre Museum curator Jacques Saunière and he's trying to stay one step ahead of the people who are trying to kill him.

The Netflix TV series *Lupin* also did this very well. The hero, Assane Diop, is trying to steal a priceless diamond necklace, but the audience soon discovers that the necklace is not Diop's true goal. His father was framed for stealing that very same necklace and later died in jail, altering the trajectory of Diop's life. He knows his father was innocent, and even knows who the true culprit was, but the only way to prove it is to steal the necklace a second time in an elaborate caper that ultimately brings the truth to light.

Alfred Hitchcock coined the term "MacGuffin" to refer to the object of a heist. It's the thing that everyone in the story is after, but the audience rarely cares about its significance and sometimes the MacGuffin isn't even shown. The MacGuffin is simply a way to get the story started and to get all the characters onto the stage. It's the shiny object in the foreground while the true story goes on in the background. The object itself does not matter. Whether it's the Maltese falcon or the holy grail, the MacGuffin is just a means to get the characters involved so they can tell the real story with the true stakes.

Employment

Everyone has a job, and we're either trying to move up the corporate ladder or we're just trying to get through the day. So you'd think that employment—seeking a job or seeking a promotion—would be great stakes for a novel. Everyone wants success and the loss of a career is devastating, right? But much like the money stakes, there isn't enough here to hang an entire novel on. After all, if your protagonist loses this job, she can get another.

Ask yourself *why* your heroine wants this job. What does

it mean to her? Why this job and not another? Maybe your heroine wants to be a lawyer because her dad always wanted to be a lawyer but couldn't afford law school. He worked two jobs so she could go, and now she feels like she owes it to the family. There could be issues of guilt, loyalty, and legacy to unpack. Or perhaps your hero wants to be an actor because he was severely bullied for a stutter while in school and he wants to prove he's overcome it by performing Shakespeare in front of live audiences. Look for the *true* stakes hidden behind the job or the promotion. Make sure the reader understands what's truly at stake for your heroine.

In *One for the Money* by Janet Evanovich, Stephanie Plum is trying to become a bounty hunter in the macho world of law enforcement in New Jersey. She's gone after the highest prize possible—police officer Joe Morelli. But the job isn't really the issue. The issue is Stephanie's self-worth. She's divorced and childless, so her parents think she's a failure. Her peers think she's just playing at this role. Nobody in Trenton believes a woman can be a bounty hunter. If Stephanie can bring in Morelli, she can prove them all wrong. Catching Morelli will prove to everyone that she's tough, smart, and can handle anything the world throws at her. Most of all, she needs to prove it to herself.

Similarly, in *The Devil Wears Prada* by Lauren Weisberger, Andi is trying to prove that she belongs in New York City, that she belongs in the world of magazine writing, and that she's "made it" in a city that's notoriously tough to make it in. Her job at *Runway* magazine is a means to realize the true stakes—Andi's sense of self.

. . .

Regret

Regret comes in two forms. The first is that your heroine tried to get something in the past and didn't get it. Now she wants it more. The second is that she did something in the past she wishes she hadn't done, or she hurt someone, and now she wants to make up for it. Regret can work well when used as a booster to another kind of stakes that matter more, but by itself, it's too weak to hold up the narrative of an entire novel.

To see why, let's look at a hypothetical example. Let's pretend you're writing a novel about a runner who wants to win the New York City marathon. Let's also pretend that your heroine entered the race last year but didn't train properly, so she didn't finish. She has regret about that, so this year, she's doing things differently. She's got a new coach, a new diet, and a new training regimen. This shows how important her goal is to her. She sacrifices parties and sleep and family time in order to go on long runs. If she loses, it means all her training was for nothing. That will feel like a death to her. If you were writing this, it would seem as if you have all the ingredients you need for the external stakes. However, some crucial things are missing.

Even if you add compelling internal stakes and personal stakes, this premise still won't work as the backbone of your novel. Why? Because the New York City marathon is run every single year. If your heroine fails, she can try next year, and the year after that. Moreover, you've already shown that your heroine can fail and survive. In many ways, that failure —and the regret it brought—made her stronger than ever.

Even though regret *by itself* isn't enough, it *is* an ingredient in many successful novels. It's not the main driver of the action, but it's a factor that affects everything the hero does.

The trick is to make the new situation similar to the old one but not exactly the same. Think echoes, not replays. Solving the new problem won't make up for what happened in the past, but the emotions are so similar that your heroine can't help but be reminded of what happened back then. She knows that nothing can change the past, but perhaps she can put some demons to rest by overcoming this new challenge. Everything that led to the failure in the past is still inside the heroine in the present, and it might stop her from achieving her goal this time, too. She'll have to overcome those emotions once and for all if she has any hope of succeeding.

In *The Silence of the Lambs* by Thomas Harris, FBI trainee Clarise Starling is trying to rescue a senator's daughter who is in the hands of a serial killer. Clarise was sent to live on her uncle's farm as a child, and unsuccessfully tried to rescue a lamb on the day of its slaughter. That memory haunts her, and she sees parallels with the kidnapped young woman who will also be slaughtered if Clarise doesn't act. At the end of the novel, when Clarise saves the senator's daughter, she stops having nightmares about the screaming lambs.

Set Yourself Up for Success

As you're writing, always make sure that your characters are the ones driving the action. Their desires, their thoughts, and their emotions will lead them to act. This makes them seem like fully-realized characters that readers will find relatable. If you get it backwards, then the events of the plot will be forced upon your hero, and you'll end up dragging him through the story instead of letting him lead. If you've ever read a book and thought that the characterization was thin, or that the characters seemed two-dimensional, the problem might not be the undeveloped characters. It might be weak stakes. Ironically, by fixing the stakes in your story, you'll fix some character problems as well.

Always ask yourself why your hero is doing what he's doing. He needs a powerful goal and the agency to act on that goal. Set yourself up for success by using a premise with built-in stakes and by choosing stakes that are strong enough to carry you through an entire novel.

EIGHT

Stakes and Minor Characters

When there's something at stake, there will be conflict, and the source of that conflict is other characters. The main conflict is between hero and villain, and that's what you'll be spending the most time on. However, minor characters are also a source of conflict, even when they are allies of the hero.

Characters are partly defined by their relationship to others. Who do they care about? Who cares about them? Who will they sacrifice for? Who will come to their aid? Who keeps their secrets?

When the true stakes are revealed at midpoint and the hero starts working toward the true goal, or solving the true problem, companions and sidekicks can either help or hinder him. And often, they seem to do one of those things while actually doing the other. Minor characters can also act as cautionary tales, can be the voice of reason or of conscience, and can affect the plot directly in multiple ways.

· · ·

Antagonist

The external stakes are what the hero wants. The antagonist is who's keeping him from getting it. Without the antagonist thwarting the hero at every turn, the story would go nowhere, and there would be no plot, no change, and no growth for the hero. Therefore, the more powerful your antagonist, the better your novel will be.

Your antagonist should have a strong goal and be highly motivated to act. Give him good reasons for doing what he does. They don't have to be honorable reasons. They probably go against everything the hero stands for, but those reasons make sense to the antagonist. The antagonist also thinks that his goal is worth sacrificing for, although he's only willing to sacrifice other people, not himself.

Give your antagonist lots of page time. This is easy to do in a romance or a family drama. It's harder to do in a thriller or a classic murder mystery. However, it's essential to get your antagonist on the page and in your hero's face as much as possible, because an enemy you can't see is an enemy you can't fight.

Hidden evil won't increase the tension the way in-your-face evil will. As you're writing, think about ways to raise the stakes by making your antagonist more annoying, more powerful, and more present. Every encounter between the protagonist and the antagonist should be more tense than the one before it, raising the stakes each time.

The external stakes are concrete things, and therefore, your antagonist must be a person, or at least personified. Your antagonist can't be an abstract thing like organized religion or guilt or corruption. If that's what your hero is fighting, your book will never end. You could fight against corruption your entire life and never be done. Even if your hero is fighting against an institution such as a government or a school, there needs to be one person who embodies that institution. In *The Hunger Games* trilogy, Katniss is fighting an evil system, but it's personified by President Snow. He's the one to beat.

In rare cases, the antagonist can be a force of nature, but even then, it's personified. In *The Martian* by Andy Weir, Mark Watney's antagonist is the planet Mars, but he's made it personal. He frequently says, "This planet is trying to kill me." He's given his antagonist a goal. Watney delights in flipping Mars the bird, as if it could see and understand the gesture. He also enjoys leaving his body waste on the ground —making Mars eat shit. The author has done a great job making the reader think that Mars is out to get Watney, and the feeling is mutual.

The Believer

Can you imagine your favorite hero without his best friend? Where would Frodo be without Sam? Or Sherlock without Watson? Or Phryne Fisher without Dot? The Believer is the hero's sidekick. This is the person who believes in the hero's mission, and believes the hero is the only one who can accomplish it. They understand the hero's needs, understand the story stakes, and stand ready to help the hero achieve his goals. This person can also provide information, support, and supplies, or act as the hero's protector.

Being an ally doesn't mean they kiss the hero's backside or let him get away with bad behavior. The believer often acts as a moral compass for the hero, letting him know when he's acting against his own values.

The Lightning Thief by Rick Riordan is about 12-year-old Percy Jackson, a demigod whose mom is mortal, but whose dad is Poseidon. When Zeus' lightning bolt is stolen, Percy has to find it and return it before the Olympian gods go to war, which would destroy the human world. Percy's friend Grover is one of two companions for this quest. Grover acts as the believer. He would do anything for Percy, and even though this is Percy's quest, Grover is just as invested in completing it. He gives Percy information, makes travel arrangements, and talks to animals on Percy's behalf. As the quest gets more dangerous, Grover never wavers in his support, even when he's terrified. He's nearly drowned, almost turned into stone, and barely escapes being eaten by a hellhound. And yet, at the climax, when Percy has three chances to escape hell but four friends to save, Grover volunteers to stay behind.

In *The Princess Bride* by William Goldman, Inigo and Fezzik start out as Westley's adversaries, but the three soon team up to try to save Buttercup from the evil prince. Fezzik is the believer. He believes in both Inigo and Westley, and is cheered by any incremental progress they make. He very much wants his team to win, whatever team that might be in the moment, and will help in whatever way is needed, whether that's lighting his cloak on fire to scare off palace guards or stealing horses to get away.

Mentors also fall under the umbrella of believers. They know how high the stakes are. They also know the hero isn't ready for what lies ahead, but they believe that he *will* be ready if the mentor gives him proper training, education, and advice. In *How to Train Your Dragon* by Cressida Cowell, Hiccup's grandfather, Old Wrinkly, is always on hand to give advice and support. When Hiccup is having trouble learning how to train a dragon, Old Wrinkly recommends different methods to try. When Hiccup whines about not wanting to be a hero, Old Wrinkly reminds him that he can find his own path to heroism. Old Wrinkly is sure that Hiccup is going to be a great leader one day, and he will be on hand to advise his grandson the whole time, even if Hiccup hates his advice.

The Doubter

The doubter is a different kind of ally. They're still on the hero's side, but they have doubts. Lots of doubts. This comes from a good place, because the doubter usually thinks they know a better way to accomplish this goal—or perhaps a better goal, period. The doubter is the friend who asks, "Are you sure you want to do that?" right before the hero tries something dangerous. The doubter wants to take a step back, think things through, and perhaps retreat. They can also be the one who lures the hero off his chosen path via distraction, either by pushing their own needs to the forefront or by dangling a different goal in front of the hero.

In *The Lightning Thief* by Rick Riordan, Annabeth is Percy's other companion on his quest to retrieve Zeus' lightning bolt. Annabeth is the doubter. She's also a demigod, but she's the daughter of Athena, the goddess of wisdom, and therefore always thinks she knows best. If Percy comes up with a plan, she's got a better one. If he knows something, she knows more. If he does something good, she thinks he should have done it sooner. Annabeth is all-in on Percy's quest, but she has definite ideas about *how* that quest should be accomplished, and is certain that everyone would be happier if they did things her way. To be fair, she's usually right about things. It's her doubt that saves them from being turned into stone by Medusa, and when Percy wants to jump off a boat, she stops him from leaping until the exact right moment, so as not to get smashed onto rocks.

In *The Princess Bride* by William Goldman, Inigo is the voice of doubt. He wants to storm the castle as much as Westley does, but he wants to know exactly *how* they're going to do it, and once they do, how they will regroup and get away. He's also got a story arc of his own, since he's been working for twenty years to get revenge for his father's death, but he has no expectation that he'll be able to succeed now that the moment is at hand. He's willing to die trying, though, if that's what it will take.

Push and Pull

In many young adult novels, it's common for the hero to have two best friends. Think of cynical Isaac and romantic Augustus in *The Fault in Our Stars* by John Green. Or gung-ho George and timid Bess in the Nancy Drew books by Carolyn Keene. Or cautious Tzain and impulsive Amari in *Children of Blood and Bone* by Tomi Adeyemi. One friend plays the role of the believer, one plays the role of the doubter, and they provide a lot of the push and pull that happens in act two.

You also see this dynamic in romance novels, where the heroine has two besties—one pushing her toward the hero, and one away from him. This raises the stakes by having the heroine constantly pulled in two directions. She loves and trusts both of her friends, but they can't both be right. In the end, the hero will level-up to be worthy of her, and she'll change as well. But in the middle of the novel, the choice isn't clear-cut and the heroine will feel like one of her friends must be wrong, if she could only figure out which one.

In The Lightning Thief by Rick Riordan, Percy Jackson likes and respects both of his friends, and knows they have experience and information that he does not. But he spends the middle of the novel like an emotional pinball being batted back and forth between Grover and Annabeth. As the trio approaches the underworld, Percy reminds his friends to stick to their plan. Grover immediately says, "I love the plan," while Annabeth asks, "What happens if the plan doesn't work?" Grover trusts that Percy knows what he's doing. Annabeth is on his side too, but she wants to know why they're moving ahead with plan A without having a plan B.

This is exactly what minor characters should be doing in your novel—either pushing the hero onward or making him justify every choice he makes. Of course you want your protagonist to have supportive friends, but think about having at least one friend who second-guesses what the hero does. These story stakes are going to change everything, and the doubter wants the hero to be absolutely sure it's worth it.

In a way, these two characters are the outward embodiment of the voices inside the hero. The believer is the voice of the external stakes, pushing forward, while the doubter is the voice of the internal stakes, holding back. This dynamic will provide a lot of tension in act two of your novel.

The Cautionary Tale

A minor character can also act as a cautionary tale for the hero. A friend or an ally might be facing similar stakes, but he's made different choices, and those choices end very badly. If the hero isn't careful, the same thing could happen to him. The hero's allies and friends are usually in the same cohort as he is. They are classmates, co-workers, or peers in the community, so it's believable that these characters are facing similar struggles.

Having another character act as a mirror is an excellent way to make the hero's abstract stakes feel more concrete. He doesn't have to guess the possible outcome of his choices when he's got an example standing right in front of him. This is a way to *show* the stakes without *telling* the reader.

In chapter two, we talked about *The White Tiger* by Aravind Adiga, and Balram's race against time. Will he get enough money to live independently before his grandmother marries him off? But those stakes would only be an abstract idea if it weren't for his older brother. Balram doesn't have to guess what will happen if his grandmother gets her way. He knows. Balram's brother has already gone down that path. He got married, now he has children to care for, and he's never getting out of that little village. Balram can see his brother's light getting dimmer by the day. By using the character of the older brother, the author has turned Balram's abstract fear into a concrete reality, and raised the stakes.

Bird Box by Josh Malerman is filled with more horrific cautionary tales. Very early in the novel, the danger is brought close to home. Malorie is hiding from the creatures, sheltering in place with her sister Shannon behind blocked windows and locked doors. However, the sisters don't cover the windows thoroughly enough, and Shannon kills herself after seeing one of the creatures. Malorie then flees to a house of other survivors, where she is safe for now, but Shannon is never far from her mind. The stakes are perfectly clear at this point. Malorie knows that she has to remain completely blind at all times, as one small mistake can cost her life.

The Sacrifice

Bird Box is an example of an author taking the cautionary tale all the way to its worst possible outcome by killing a minor character. It happens frequently in thrillers, mysteries, fantasy novels, science fiction, and horror. A minor character dies so the reader knows how dangerous the situation is for the heroine.

This can be done well or it can be done poorly. The worst is when the love interest is killed simply so the reader will hate the antagonist more. This is known as "fridging the girl-friend," and it's been done so often, and so poorly, that it's become a cliche. If the only reason your female character, or child, or beloved pet exists is so she can die and thus motivate the hero to seek revenge, you've got some rewriting to do.

But the death of a minor character can also be done well. It can have meaning beyond just the shock factor or a way to make readers cry. A character death can spin the plot in a new direction, with true consequences for the other characters. It can also deepen the theme, and it can enrich characterization. How will this death change your hero? And did the minor character simply die, or did he take a bullet for someone? That kind of scene can add a tasty serving of guilt on top of the hero's motivation to fight harder.

In *The Lord of the Rings* by J.R.R. Tolkien, the wizard Gandalf is the wise guide who is leading the fellowship on their quest to destroy the one ring. The group is traveling through an unused mine that some dwarves had to abandon because they dug too deep and unleashed a terrifying creature called a balrog. Gandalf places himself between the fellowship and the balrog, sacrificing himself and allowing the others to escape unharmed. Gandalf was a friend and mentor, respected and loved by everyone in the fellowship. His death is not only sad, but it makes the quest more difficult, because now their party is unbalanced. Frodo and the other hobbits have heart, while the humans, dwarf, and elf provide plenty of muscle, but the brain of their operation is gone. Moreover, the quest seems that much more dangerous, now that the readers know there are creatures so powerful, they can kill a wizard like Gandalf. The author knew what he was doing by killing off this minor character at this exact moment, and he got the maximum mileage out of it.

NINE

Increasing Tension

The goal of an author is to force readers to keep turning the pages. Your readers have become invested via the personal stakes, and you've shocked them at the midpoint with the reveal of the true stakes. They're waiting for the other shoe to drop via the internal stakes. But is every scene in your novel as tension-filled as you can make it?

You want to make sure that readers *can't* stop reading. You want them to miss their bus stop, stay up past their bedtimes, and immediately click "buy" on the next book in the series. You do that by making the stakes deeper while increasing the tension at every turn.

After you've upped the stakes at the big turning points, it's time to look at the other scenes in your novel. These smaller scenes might not have the world-altering revelations or the big shootouts, but you'll still want to make sure the tension increases page by page. If you can make those smaller moments just as gripping as the bigger ones, your reader won't be able to put your book down until the very last page—after which she'll recommend your novel to all her friends.

You don't have to do all of these things, and they don't have to be in every scene. But if your story is dragging or your beta readers say your pacing is off, consider trying some of these techniques to up the tension in your story.

Making Things Worse

Early in the novel, you've made the stakes very clear, but once isn't enough. Make sure to periodically remind readers why the heroine is working toward this goal and what she will lose if she fails. The *worst* way to do this is in dialogue. The heroine's friends and enemies already know what's at stake because they're either helping her or thwarting her. People don't usually tell each other things they already know, so to have the heroine discuss exactly what's at stake over and over will not ring true. Far better to remind the reader through objects, images, and thoughts. In thrillers, you can periodically cut away to the villain, to show him using his power, so the reader knows what the hero is up against. You can show victims suffering if the hero doesn't act.

But there are other ways to remind the reader why the heroine is doing what she does, even in stories where the stakes aren't life-threatening. In *Girl with a Pearl Earring* by Tracy Chevalier, Griet is a live-in maid in the household of the painter Vermeer. She didn't want this job, but had no choice but to take it after her father was blinded in an accident at his tile factory. Her mother is taking care of her father and younger sister full time, so Griet's salary is the family's only income. Even though Griet is separated from her family, she is reminded of them at every turn. When she sees the tiles in her new employer's kitchen, she looks to see if any of them came from her father's factory. When she goes to the butcher shop, she thinks about how long it's been since her family has been able to afford meat. Vermeer's young daughters remind her of her sister. Griet's workload is grueling and her living conditions harsh, but she bears it all for many years. The reader understands why she puts up with it, because the author has sprinkled reminders in every chapter.

In addition to having a large, overarching goal for the novel, your hero should also have smaller goals along the way. He should begin every scene by wanting something and having some idea how to get it. Just as you had to be crystal clear when telling the reader the story goal, you also have to tell the reader what the scene goal is. What does your hero want at this exact moment in time? What steps is he taking in the pursuit of his larger goal? Each scene will then either end with a disaster, as the hero didn't get what he wanted, or a victory that comes with a caveat. If the start of the scene is a question, "Will my hero succeed on this next step toward his goal?" The answer needs to be either "No, and..." or "Yes, but..."

A great example of this principle in action is *The Martian* by Andy Weir. Astronaut Mark Watney makes plan after plan to survive on Mars and eventually leave it. But every problem he solves along the way brings up a new one. Watney's crew is returning for him, but he'll have to make a long journey in a rover to get to the pick-up point. First, he has to make the rover into a mini habitat so he can survive the journey. Then he has to think about power, so he rigs up a battery and a spare, but he has no place to put them. He finally rigs up the batteries on a harness outside his rover, but he'll have to put on a spacesuit every time he needs to swap batteries. He tries a test drive, but barely lasts an hour before nearly freezing to death. He needs heat to survive the trip, but diverting energy to heat means less fuel to move. This progression continues through the book, as everything Watney tries either fails or raises more problems. Readers were riveted, and this novel soared up the bestseller list because the author never let his hero catch a break. When you're writing, you need to be just as mean to your own characters.

Another way to make things worse is to decrease the hero's power. He has a goal, and he's doing everything he can to accomplish it, but he's running out of something. It could be fuel, resources, energy, transportation, willpower, or someone else's patience. The hero has one chance to reach his goal and a finite amount of time to do it in, but you can amplify this idea by also taking away the very thing he needs to get it done. If you're writing an extended chase scene, you can have the hero running out of gas. If you're writing a murder mystery, you can make the most important witness refuse to talk to the detective. If you're writing a YA novel where the hero is in trouble at school, you can give him a principal who won't listen to his very good reasons for standing up for himself.

In the novel *Jurassic Park* by Michael Crichton, Dr. Grant and his friends are trying to get away from carnivorous dinosaurs who have escaped from their cages. They have two small children with them, which means they have an extra burden while running or fighting, since kids can't run fast or fight hard. Grant's attention is always split between fighting the dinosaurs and protecting the children. The power has been cut from the island as well. Getting it back on won't cage the dinosaurs but at least they can call for help. Or can they? A hurricane is sweeping the island, so no help will be able to get to the humans trapped there. No matter what happens in *Jurassic Park*, the author always finds a way to make it worse. This is the kind of tension that will keep readers glued to the page, not just at the big turning points, but in every scene.

Tension in Small Moments

Beware of "set up" scenes where you're introducing characters or moving them from here to there so they can be in the right place for something cool to happen later. Too often these become travelogues, listing the streets a hero drives on or the landmarks he passes on the way. Or a hero will go through his whole morning routine where nothing happens, just so he can arrive at work where the real action begins. Some of these scenes can be cut. But if you can't cut them, you can infuse tension into these scenes by having your hero be late for something, or worried about something, or better yet, give him a goal—even a tiny one.

In the first chapter of *One for the Money* by Janet

Evanovich, Stephanie Plum is on her way to her parents' house for dinner. It could have been a very flat and boring scene. It's an ordinary day in an ordinary neighborhood in anticipation of an ordinary family dinner. Stephanie even knows what's on the menu, since her mother cooks pot roast and potatoes every Sunday. But the author ups the tension by having Stephanie followed by the repo man who wants to impound her car. Stephanie is six months behind on her car payments and she knows it's only a matter of time before it's repossessed. Worse, the recovery agent is her old high school classmate and a major creep, who offers to let her keep the car in exchange for sexual favors.

The author has turned what could have been a "useless" scene into a necessary one. It's dramatic, as Stephanie tries to bargain for her car. It's thematic, since she is about to go into a similar line of work herself. It shows what terrible financial straits she's in. And it fits the tone of the book because the scene itself is funny.

If you stop the forward momentum of the story for long passages of description, it will kill the tension in your novel, especially if the description lies flat on the page without any depth to it. You can add extra dimension to every bit of description by infusing it with contradictions and character voice. Nobody feels purely one way about anything. You might have a favorite chair, but wish it were just a little bit shorter so your legs could stretch out. Or you might love key lime pie, but wish it weren't so high in sugar so you could eat it more often. You might hate living in New York City with its noise and expense and pollution, but at least there are great restaurants all around you. By adding both the positive and the negative, you're building in tiny bits of tension that makes a static piece of description feel active and interesting on the page. And remember that description isn't *your* opinion, it's your *character's* opinion. The more you can infuse it with a unique point of view, the better.

Where'd You Go, Bernadette by Maria Semple is about Bernadette Fox, who lives with her family in a dilapidated house in Seattle, on property overgrown with blackberry vines—which contribute to a major plot point. The vines are growing *inside* the house, bumping up through the carpet and under floorboards rotted by all of Seattle's rain. Bernadette's teenage daughter knows the vines are a problem. Some of her friends won't spend the night because they are so creeped out by the blackberries growing into the house. But at the same time, she loves the vines because she sees them as protection. She thinks of Sleeping Beauty, and the way the walls of briars kept her safe while she slept for a hundred years. By presenting both sides, the author has made the description dynamic and filled with tension.

Bernadette was once an architect, and she also has opinions about the vines. The house they live in was supposed to be her passion project, but a series of miscarriages followed by the birth of her very frail daughter drained all her energy. The blackberry vines are a symbol of her lost ambition, and she doesn't have the capacity to deal with them. She feels overwhelmed and guilty about the vines, but also helpless against them. By attaching emotion and opinion, the author has turned flat description into something dynamic.

When you're writing, look for places that seem to drag or scenes that your beta readers say move too slowly. Is your description doing all it can? Description and exposition are necessary to all novels, but they don't have to be detached and flat. They can ripple with tension. What does your point-of-view character think about this thing? What are the contradictory feelings he has about it? Put both sides of the description onto the page as often as you can.

Increasing Emotion

The hotspots in your novel—those big turning point scenes at the end of each act—are already filled with emotion. Dramatic things are happening and your hero feels very deeply about them. But what about the other scenes in the novel? Are you pulling every last drop of emotion out of each scene? Readers are reading to have an emotional experience, and the more you can deliver it to them, the more they will love your novel.

Don't neglect your protagonist's internal stakes while you're racing her through the plot. Although the internal stakes are bubbling below the surface for most of the novel, you need to have some of those bubbles rise to the surface and pop. You do this by letting the other characters take small swipes at the heroine's internal stakes. If she needs to forgive someone, make the other party more unforgivable. If she has trust issues, plant doubt. If the internal stakes are self-worth, let the other characters treat her self-esteem like a pin cushion.

In *One for the Money* by Janet Evanovich, every time Stephanie visits her family, they take little digs at her. Her mother tells her she'll never get married if she doesn't start dressing nicer. Her father thinks she only deserves a mini-mum-wage job. And her grandmother wonders if *she* should be a bounty hunter too. After all, if Stephanie can do it, how hard could it be? Over and over, they express the values of their tight-knit Trenton suburb, and constantly tell Stephanie she isn't measuring up. The irony is, her family is only saying out loud what she's been saying quietly to herself. Patching the holes in Stephanie's self-worth is going to take a lot of work, and capturing a big bounty will help her do that.

Another way to increase emotion is by turning the public's eye on your characters. Things that seem uncomfort-able or annoying in private can become a full-blown crisis by making them public. Books about fictional celebrities, from rock stars to reality TV contestants, are hugely popular. We also love to read about royal families in fictional kingdoms. But books don't have to have larger-than-life settings to have this same effect. Small towns and high schools can be equally uncomfortable when everyone is up in everyone else's busi-ness and the gossip mill is churning.

When you're writing, look at the scenes in your novel that take place in private. Can you move any of those scenes to a public place? Perhaps the couple on the brink of divorce doesn't fight in their kitchen, but at a PTO meeting. Maybe the hero has to apologize to the woman of his dreams, but not on her front porch. Perhaps instead he has to grovel in front of all the co-workers and customers of the ice cream parlor where she works. Is your heroine going to her gynecologist to confirm her at-home pregnancy test? Are the receptionist, the nurse, and the parking lot attendant all people she knows, so she can't keep the news to herself even if she wants to?

Humans are intensely social animals, so put as many people as you can into the most awkward scenes in your novel. It will make even the smallest scenes feel like the stakes are higher, since your characters will do almost anything to avoid public humiliation.

In *Dork Diaries* by Rachel Renée Russell, Nikki is the new kid at a snobby private middle school. She's desperate to fit in, but everything she does backfires as she suffers through one embarrassing situation after another. She's snubbed in the lunchroom, talked about in the halls, and at the all-is-lost moment, her prized painting for the school art show is ruined, right in front of the snottiest girls in school. The author did a brilliant job of amplifying Nikki's trauma by giving her no privacy to recover. Nikki has to face her nemesis in front of everyone she knows while her emotions are boiling.

Readers don't quite trust success that comes too easily. If your hero has a goal, and works toward that goal, and then achieves that goal, it feels too simple, even if the hero is working his tail off and trying his very best. Effort isn't enough. The hero can fight with all he's got, but if it didn't hurt, readers won't care.

The way to ramp up tension is by making sure two steps forward is followed by one step back, and that one step back hurts like hell. The more the hero suffers on his quest, the more the readers assume he "deserves" to win. This is a hard thing for many writers to do. We love our heroes a lot and we hate to see them suffer. Some writers only let their heroes suffer a little bit. Others only let them suffer for a short time, bailing them out of trouble at the first opportunity. But I'd encourage you to go deep and let your hero feel terrible for as long as you can stand it—and then longer still. I'm not advocating for "misery porn." Some books are just unrelentingly bleak and therefore no fun to read. Far better to make a jagged sawtooth pattern—one happy scene for each couple of downers, sliding ever closer to the all-is-lost moment, when you'll bring your hero as low as possible. Because the more the hero suffers, the sweeter the victory at the end.

The Lord of the Rings by J.R.R. Tolkien is a huge saga, spanning three thick books, where it takes the efforts of nearly an entire kingdom to overthrow an evil ruler. It all centers on one small hobbit named Frodo on a quest to throw a cursed ring into Mount Doom, where it will be destroyed. Frodo walks endless miles and fights off unimaginably terrifying creatures including wraiths, orcs, and a giant spider. His mentor leaves him, he is betrayed by those he thought were his friends, and by the end, he's starving, exhausted, and ready to die. And yet, it isn't all doom and gloom. There are pockets of rest for Frodo, times when allies come to his aid, moments of beauty, and the companionship of the best friend anyone could ever ask for. Readers are overjoyed when Frodo is victorious. He has worked so hard and suffered so much that it only seems right that he wins. At the same time, the story isn't so bleak that readers stopped reading it. That up-and-down progression keeps readers going through many hundreds of pages.

One version of suffering that readers respond strongly to is injustice. Has your heroine been wronged in some way? Has she been accused of something she hasn't done? Unfairly punished? There are many ways to stir reader emotions and bond readers to your characters, but this is one of the strongest. Perhaps it's because we've all been there. We've all had our words twisted, been disliked for no reason, or had our motives questioned. At one time or another, we've all felt like the underdog, with a situation that's set up for us to fail. When this happens to characters we love, our hearts break for them.

In *Girl with a Pearl Earring* by Tracy Chevalier, Griet owns only two personal possessions other than her clothing—a tile painted by her father and a hair comb made of tortoise-shell. The comb is similar to one that Vermeer's wife owns, and one of the children switches the two when Griet isn't looking. Griet is immediately accused of theft, since it's always assumed that maids steal things. Nothing Griet can say will prove her innocence, and it's only when Vermeer himself gets involved that the truth comes to light. But even when the comb is found and the child punished, Griet is *still* under suspicion by everyone in the household, as they all assume that Vermeer took Griet's side because he's sleeping with her. Why else would a gentleman come to the aid of a mere maid? She's not sleeping with her boss, but Griet's reputation is ruined anyway, and it's the beginning of the end of her job in Vermeer's household.

Your heroine is facing a difficult problem with mile-high stakes, and it's only human to want to quit. Your heroine should be dragged forward, feeling she has no choice. The stakes are high enough that she *won't* quit, but she might be *tempted* to do so. If the heroine wishes she could quit, and has good reasons to quit, but sticks with things anyway, it makes it all the more heroic. And if she keeps on fighting for the sake of another person? Readers will cheer.

In *Dumplin'* by Julie Murphy, Willowdean enters her mom's beauty pageant partly as a joke, partly to make a statement, and partly to make her mom mad. As soon as she enters the pageant, three other girls from her school sign up too. The three of them are all misfits in their own ways, and not beauty pageant material at all, but seeing Willowdean enter the pageant gives them the courage to do so as well. When things get hard, and Willowdean considers dropping out of the pageant, her three new friends are upset. They tell her that if she drops out, they'll drop out too. How can Willowdean let those other girls down? She has to follow through and actually try to win.

Emotions in Conflict

Did you ever have a tough decision to make? Did you ever have things pulling you in two directions? What if both of those directions are equally good? Or equally bad? It's torture, isn't it?

Emotion is the fuel that's pushing your readers through the story, and the most powerful fuel is emotions in conflict. The tension isn't in the emotions themselves but in the hesitation and indecision they create in the character. When a character has mixed emotions about something, that means a decision will need to be made. The reader can't help but wonder what that decision will be, so she turns the page to find out.

You're already doing this on a macro scale. You've given your hero big stakes that he doesn't want to face but feels compelled to tackle. Meanwhile, he has a friend who believes in him pushing him forward while a friend who doubts is questioning his every move. But you can also do this on a micro level. Each step on the hero's journey, no matter how small, is accompanied by mixed emotions.

Let's say you're writing a cozy mystery and your amateur detective is trying to solve a murder. In cozies, the sleuth usually knows all the suspects. She has to investigate people she likes and trusts, so each conversation will be a minefield. She wants to believe what her neighbor or co-worker is telling her, but the facts just don't add up. Can she ask the tough questions without alienating a friend? How far can she push someone to tell the truth?

Or perhaps you're writing a thriller where the hero is on the run from people who are trying to kill him, while simultaneously trying to protect his family. Should he run, or should he hide in place? And will hesitating over this choice cost him precious time?

Or maybe you're writing a Regency romance novel, where the hero is known as a scoundrel and a rake who ruins women. He's also attractive, socially connected, and oh-so sweet when the hero and heroine are alone. Should the heroine believe the gossip that surrounds him, or take him at face value? Every conversation between the two main characters will dance around these mixed feelings, adding tension to every scene.

In *The White Tiger* by Aravind Adiga, Balram is desperate to rise above his circumstances, and one day, he makes a trial run at it by daring himself to go to the mall. The mall has security at every door, and servants are not allowed, so Balram first has to dress the part. He buys clothes that resemble his boss' outfits and grooms himself like a rich man. He makes it inside the mall, but as he walks around, he feels the eyes of the guards on him, making him skittish. He can't enjoy this new experience because he's sure he's going to be kicked out at any moment. And all he can think about while he's inside is his peers. He wonders what the other drivers in his social circle would say if they could see him now. He wants to tell them all about it, but he fears their mockery. Once safely outside, he rushes to the other drivers, but when he's among them, he becomes mute. He can't tell them what he's done because they wouldn't understand what it meant to him.

This small scene is bursting with contradictory emotions. Balram is sure his plan will work, but scared that he'll be found out. He wants to fit in with the upper classes, but feels more comfortable with the other servants. He's thrilled at what he's gotten away with, yet shy about bragging on it. Readers understand how Balram can feel two opposite emotions at the same time, and they feel the tension he feels. Readers want him to stay inside the mall, to enjoy the air-conditioning and good smells. They want Balram to be able to feel like a rich man for once in his life. And they're also worried. What if he gets caught? What if he's kicked out and humiliated in front of the other drivers?

It's a small scene, and the plot doesn't hinge on it. And yet, readers turn the pages, eager to know what will happen. That's the power of emotions in conflict. When you're writing, look for places to add complexity to your hero's inner world. He's going to have many decisions to make, both big and small. Add weight to those decisions by making them harder. Don't worry that you're going to confuse your reader. Humans are great at looking at all sides of an issue, and emotions are very often layered on top of one another. Your fictional hero can be equally complex, adding richness to otherwise flat scenes.

TEN

Resolving the Stakes

If you're having trouble finishing your novel, it's often because the stakes aren't clear enough. When the author is crystal clear on the story stakes, and they are important and meaningful with a solid deadline, then writing the ending of the novel is more straightforward. At the all-is-lost moment, the internal stakes and the external stakes collide, and the hero has a wake-up call. Now, finally, he knows how to fix his problem or reach his goal. The climax is where the external stakes are resolved.

This is the emotional payoff the reader has been sticking around for, so don't rush it. Don't jump right into the final battle. Build it up a little, prolong your hero's agony for as long as you can. The final quarter of the book has a lot of work to do. You're going to answer every vital story question and resolve every important problem. This section of your story deserves all the drama you can wring out of it.

. . .

What an Ending Must Do

First, a novel has to actually *end*, not just stop. Modern readers demand a definitive ending. You have to show victory or defeat, and you have to show how the hero's life has changed after going through this experience. Things can't just taper off. No matter how pretty your language or how much you want your novel to be "realistic" or "slice of life," things must come to a high point, after which things change forever.

There are many ways to tie off loose ends. The best way is to resolve all the subplots and any other minor plot points *before* the climax scene. But that isn't always possible. So the very last chance to do it is in the resolution—the little scene that happens after the climax. There, you can answer any lingering questions.

Even if you're writing book one or book two in a longer series, your novel still has to stand alone in some sense. You can leave a few things unresolved, and scatter a few bread-crumbs for the next book in the series, but the main problem in *this* novel needs to be dealt with. There needs to be a conclusion that shows how things have changed. Readers need to know they can close this book and be emotionally okay until the next book starts.

To All the Boys I've Loved Before by Jenny Han is the first book in a trilogy. In this young adult novel, Lara Jean's secret love letters accidentally get mailed to five boys. Lara Jean tries to hide her true crush by inventing a fake relation-ship with the most popular boy in school. By the end of the novel, everything has worked out. Her fake relationship has become real, she's back on good terms with both of her sisters, and the mortifying truth that she once had a crush on her sister's boyfriend has been left in the past. The author sewed up all the major conflicts of this book while leaving a few things open for the next one. In book two, a boy who received one of Lara Jean's letters comes back into her life, creating a love triangle. It was just enough conflict to carry readers over from book one into book two without ending book one with a cliffhanger.

An ending has to be earned, not given. Whatever happens at the end of a story has to grow naturally out of what came before. There should be no sudden breaks in logic, no weird coincidences, and no *deus ex machina*. Your hero can't be saved by other people or convenient weapons or ideas that show up out of the blue. Whatever resources he's got going into the final confrontation is all he's got, and what happens next is the natural consequence of events that came before.

The ultimate goal for all of our novel endings is that they are satisfying. Most of the time this means victory for the heroine. She battles the forces of evil—whether that's hostile aliens trying to take over Earth or her bratty little brother who won't stay out of her room—and emerges victorious. However, an ending doesn't necessarily have to be happy. A mixed ending or a sad ending can also be satisfying as long as the stakes are resolved. The reader needs to feel like the journey she's been on with this character has been worth it.

At the ending of *The Devil Wears Prada* by Lauren Weisberger, Andi yells at her boss in front of the entire fashion world at an important runway show. It's a genre-appropriate, direct confrontation. Andi then quits her job, leaves New York, and kind of gives up on magazine writing. She moves back in with her parents and sells her designer clothing. It isn't until the very last pages of the novel that she returns to New York. It's a bittersweet resolution because she never fully defeats her nemesis and Miranda is as powerful as ever. But Andi realizes that she didn't need to defeat Miranda Priestly, or even last an entire year at *Runway*, in order to be successful.

Even a sad ending can be satisfying as long as the stakes are resolved one way or the other. *1984* by George Orwell is about a country where democracy has been replaced by fascism. Government agents have been trying to break the hero, Winston Smith, but he resists for most of the novel, right up to the end. The last line of the novel is, "He loved Big Brother." Winston has been broken. But it's still a satisfactory ending because *1984* is a cautionary tale. It couldn't have ended any other way. If it ended with Winston defeating the State, the reader would have nothing to fear.

A sad ending is a risk, though. Modern readers have fully embraced the idea that any hero with determination who works hard deserves happiness. So the majority of novels written in English for a Western audience have happy endings. Some genres are defined by the expectation of "happily ever after," but it's actually the unspoken expectation in *all* genre fiction. Romance ends with declarations of love, mysteries end when the crime is solved, and thrillers end with defeating the bad guy and thwarting his evil plans. If you're strongly drawn to grim stories, then you should write them. Just be aware that it will limit your audience.

. . .

Your Genre Determines Your Climax

Because the external stakes have a deadline, the hero will have to face the problem no matter what. The clearer the stakes, the better the ending of the story, and knowing the expectations of your genre really helps.

In thrillers and related genres, the hero will defeat the bad guy or be defeated by him. The hero has leveled up his skills throughout the story and is now in a position to defeat the antagonist. In *Jaws* by Peter Benchley, Brody has become stronger throughout the novel, conquering his fear of the water, so he's finally able to kill the shark. In *Misery* by Stephen King, Paul Sheldon is slowly being tortured to death by Annie Wilkes, but when he finally has his chance to kill her, he's brave enough to take it.

In other genres, such as literary fiction, there is no reason to defeat the antagonist. More often, the climax is a reconciliation with the antagonist or a new understanding of where the antagonist is coming from. In *The Joy Luck Club* by Amy Tan, the four American daughters learn to see their Chinese-born mothers in a new light, and the resolution brings new understanding between them. In *Dumplin'* by Julie Murphy, the beauty pageant is a vehicle for Willowdean and her mother to reconcile their differences.

In a romance, both of the protagonists have changed for the better. The ending is both halves of the couple realizing they were meant to be together, and because they've changed, it's possible for them to be together now. They've become worthy of one another.

No matter the genre, knowing what's at stake will help with *every* part of the novel, but especially its final chapters. With your story stakes fixed clearly in your mind, and your genre expectations providing a framework, the final act of your novel will be easier to write.

The Payoff

The climax scene is the big payoff your entire novel has been building to. You've been making promises to the reader about what to expect, and now is the time to make good on those promises. The most important thing to remember is that this is the most epic scene in your book. It should be the most exciting, with the most emotion and drama and the biggest consequences. Don't let other scenes in your novel overshadow this one.

Your hero has leveled-up to a point that he can actually win. He started the novel in a weaker position, but everything he's gone through in the story means he's finally strong enough to defeat the antagonist. You've plunged him into terrible trouble and he's had to learn some hard lessons because of that. He's taking those lessons and rising to the occasion. Now is your chance to let your hero shine. He's resolved his internal stakes, and that will allow him to emerge victorious in the final battle.

How to Train Your Dragon by Cressida Cowell is a middle-grade book about Hiccup Haddock, who is the son of a Viking chief. The chief's son is supposed to be large, fearless strong, and insensitive, but Hiccup is the opposite of that. He doesn't want to train a fierce dragon, he wants to befriend a tiny one. He's adopted the world's smallest dragon and has taught himself the dragon language so he can speak to it. He's bullied for this, and even his father is embarrassed, but Hiccup wants to make this odd partnership work. His dragon is about as easy to train as a stubborn cat, so Hiccup has to become extremely resourceful to make his dragon obey him.

At the initiation into the tribe, Hiccup fails the dragon-training test and is threatened with exile. But when huge sea dragons come ashore, threatening to eat everyone in the village, Hiccup is the only one who can talk to them. Hiccup's internal stakes are his feelings of self-worth. He doesn't feel that he measures up to the expectations of his family and his tribe. However, he's uniquely qualified to defeat the sea dragons. He becomes a leader among the other kids, and even the bullies listen to him. Hiccup is braver than he knew, and his tiny pet dragon helps him save the day.

At the climax, there must be *direct* confrontation between the protagonist and the antagonist. The external stakes are going to be resolved here, and the reader needs to see the protagonist and the antagonist face off. Be careful that you're not taking agency or choice away from your hero in subtle ways. You can't end your novel by removing the antagonist's power. That's not enough. It would solve the hero's problem, but it wouldn't satisfy the requirements for a good ending. Nor can you have the hero run away from the problem or solve it with technology. Your action hero crashed the bad guy's computer system? Drained his bank accounts? Disabled his yacht? None of that matters unless it happens on the way to a gunfight or at least a brawl between the protagonist and the antagonist. Your literary fiction heroine wrote a scathing letter to her abusive mother before running away from home? That's good, but not good enough. Readers need to hear her say these things directly to her mother. They need to see the tears in her mother's eyes and feel the door slam as the heroine leaves home forever. Readers expect a showdown and that's what you need to give them.

Similarly, make sure it's the heroine herself who solves the final problem, not her sidekick or ally. There's a reason that allies tend to fall away from the heroine near the end of stories. She needs to handle things on her own. The heroine is the one who has conquered her fears. She's the one who has leveled-up her skills. She's the one who had the epiphany at the all-is-lost moment, so she's the only one with the strength and understanding to solve this problem. Sidekicks can go after secondary antagonists. They can clear the path for the heroine, or they can assist her in taking down the bad guy, but this is a job for the heroine and she's the one that needs to deliver the final result.

The direct confrontation can be a fight with swords or a laser battle. It can also be a shouting match, or a reconciliation, or a new understanding. There can be a fight to the death. There can also be groveling and apologies. Even happy tears. Whatever your genre is asking for is okay here, as long as it's direct. The heroine will be active here. She's bringing the fight to the antagonist, so she'll be the one forcing the final encounter to take place. Earlier in the novel, things happened to the heroine and she reacted, but those internal stakes aren't holding her back anymore. The time for reacting is over and now she's on the offensive.

Whatever steps she takes here, they must be irrevocable.

It will be shown in an action. Not just a thought. Not just words. *Action.* An idea or a thought aren't enough because the heroine can always change her mind about things. She can go back on her word. But there are no backsies in fiction. Your heroine needs to take decisive action at the climax that can't be undone.

The heroine of *Mexican Gothic* by Silvia Moreno-Garcia is trapped in a house with immortal racists who want to take over her mind and then use her body for breeding purposes. Noemi has come to this isolated house to rescue her cousin, and along the way she befriends one of the house's occupants, a frail young man who wants to help her escape.

Noemi manages to get away from the immortals and bring the others with her, but mere escape isn't enough. She could get all three of them to the nearest town, and all the way back to Mexico City, where her family has money and resources. It's reasonable to think she'd be safe there. But that wouldn't be a satisfying ending. Instead, the author delivers what readers want—a direct confrontation and decisive action. Noemi has a hand-to-hand fight with her cousin's husband. She then burns the hive mind controlling the house and its occupants, and while she's at it, she burns down the house, solving the problem once and for all.

The Resolution

Now that you've written your novel up through the climax, there is still one more scene you need to write before the novel is finished. You need a resolution (or a dénouement if you're feeling fancy). The all-is-lost moment is where the internal stakes were resolved. The climax resolved the external stakes, as the hero finally reached his goal. Your hero sacrificed so much and he risked some kind of death to make this happen. The resolution is where you show that it was all worth it. What changes have come into the hero's life because of the events of the story? This is also your last chance to tie up any loose ends, and give your readers a little peek at what happily ever after looks like.

This is a great place to circle back to the personal stakes that were present at the beginning of the novel. Your heroine will see those smaller, more personal stakes with fresh eyes now. Perhaps she'll laugh at her earlier self for thinking such a trivial thing was important. Perhaps she'll have solved those personal stakes along the way. Perhaps she'll still be dealing with that same personal problem, but on a new level. She's calmer and wiser now, and she can deal with such things more easily.

In the last few pages of *The Devil Wears Prada* by Lauren Weisberger, Andi is interviewing for another magazine job in her old building. She catches a glimpse of Miranda Priestly's new assistant, who looks miserable. Nothing has changed there. Miranda is still the worst boss ever, but Andi doesn't care because she's on a whole other level now. She doesn't have to take the first job offered to her. She has options. She can hold out for a permanent job at a serious magazine with a boss who values her.

The shorter you can make your resolution scene, the better. You've just given the reader the most intense emotional experience of the book, so you should let that experience be as pure as possible by ending the book as soon as you can. Things are good for your heroine now. (Or terrible in a satisfying way if you're writing a downer ending.) Give her some validation that her actions were right and that this journey was worth it, and then end the book.

Don't underestimate your reader. If you write fully three-dimensional characters that feel like real people, the reader will easily guess what the hero's reaction to the climax will be. If your story stakes are crystal clear, the reader will know what's been achieved by solving the story problem. They know how life will be different now. Readers love anticipating things, including the fallout of big scenes, so you might not have to explain as much as you think you do.

Finally, the last page, the last paragraph, and the last sentence of your novel should contain a strong visual image. Do not leave your readers with an abstract idea or a bunch of purple prose. Use the hero's concrete action to *show* how things have changed. Your hero or heroine should do something, not just think pretty thoughts.

Emma by Jane Austen ends with two weddings. Emma's best friend marries the farmer who proposed to her in act one, and Emma finally marries Mr. Knightley. The stakes in the book were matchmaking and the search for love, and the weddings show that love has indeed been found.

At the end of *The Da Vinci Code* by Dan Brown, Langdon is kneeling in reverence before the divine feminine. He has learned through the events of the novel that those symbols he's been studying are not masculine symbols. They're feminine ones that have been erased through history. Kneeling is a powerful way to end the book.

It might take time to find the perfect action for your hero.

You'll want something that is unique, genre-appropriate, and not a cliche. And it will have to be something that your hero is likely to do. But somewhere in your story is an action that will truly show the change the protagonist has undergone. End with that.

ELEVEN

You Got This!

I hope I've given you a fresh perspective on story stakes, and inspired you to dig deeper when crafting your own stories. Perhaps I've changed your thinking about stakes in one small way. Or perhaps I've clarified something for you, or answered a question you've always wondered about. Maybe I've upended everything in your novel-in-progress.

At this point, you might be feeling overwhelmed. You might be saying, "Jesus, Alex, what did you tell us this for?" You might be thinking this is way too much information, because when you sit down to write your novel, you just want to tell a fun story about some cool people having adventures. What's wrong with that?

It's unusual to talk about stakes at this deep, specific level. And let me restate that you do *not* have to have this all figured out before you start writing. You'll figure out most of it as you go.

Use this book as a resource, but don't ever let it force you into stiff writing with rigid rules, or worse yet, crush your spirit. *Story* trumps everything. If your story is working—hitting its emotional beats and resonating with readers—then don't change it based on some arbitrary "rules" of good writing. Always be true to *your* story, making it the best story it can be, with the highest stakes possible within the bounds of the story you want to tell.

If you highlighted part of this book, covered it in post-it notes, or scribbled in the margins, that's great. I'm glad to know that this book was helpful. But please don't take this book into your writing room with you. A novel is a big thing and it's way too much to hold in your head all at once. At this point, you understand what story stakes are and how to use them. So trust yourself when you're writing—especially when you're writing a first draft.

The only things you need to know when you begin your novel are what your hero or heroine wants and how far they'll go to get it.

And how far *you* will go to put the highest, deepest, most meaningful stakes into your novel.

For Further Reading

Have you finished the first draft of your novel? Are you wondering what to do next? Don't miss *The Big-Picture Revision Checklist*, your guide to revising a novel without frustration.

The Big-Picture Revision Checklist will help you make likable protagonists who are flawed in exactly the right ways, and antagonists that readers love to hate. You'll crank up your story stakes and pinpoint the five crucial scenes every novel needs. With comprehensive explanations and examples from contemporary fiction, this clear-eyed manual gives you the tools you need to bring your book to the finish line.

Following this checklist makes revision easy, straightforward, and even fun!

The Big-Picture Revision Checklist is available in ebook, paperback, and hardcover at all online retailers and bookstores.

About the Author

Alex Kourvo loves books. She reads them, writes them, edits them, reviews them, and teaches other people how to write them. Sometimes, she dreams about books.

Alex is an editor with over a decade of experience editing for small presses and private clients. She's the co-founder of the Emerging Writers Workshop at the Ann Arbor District Library, where she gave monthly writing classes for six years. Alex's blog, *Writing Slices*, is exclusively dedicated to reviewing how-to books for writers. There are over 200 reviews on her site.

Alex lives in Michigan, in the perfect town, on the perfect street, in the perfect house. She loves key lime pie, puppies, sunbeams, and new books to read.

You can visit Alex on Twitter or Instagram, or find out more about her editing services at
AlexKourvo.com

Acknowledgments

Special thanks to Bethany, Gail, Kirsten, and Michael for valuable advice.

With a big shout out to everyone who attended the Emerging Writers Workshop at the Ann Arbor District Library. In so many ways, this book is for all of you.